© Phillip Jones 2022

The rights of Phillip Jones to be identified as the author of this work have been asserted by him in accordance with sections 77 and 78 of the Copyright, Designs and Patents Act 1988.

All rights reserved. No part of this book may be reprinted or reproduced or utilised in any form or by any electronic, mechanical, or other means, now known or hereafter invented, including photocopying and recording, or in any information storage or retrieval system, without the prior written consent of the author, the author's representatives or a licence permitting copying in the UK issued by the Copyright Licensing Agency Ltd.
www.cla.co.uk

ISBN 978-1-78222-955-1

All plate images courtesy of Getty iStock

Book design, layout and production management by Into Print
www.intoprint.net
+44 (0)1604 832140

Foreword

I hope this collection of the early works of the late Reverend James Thompson will be welcomed by all who knew this wonderful man. The text is unaltered and every effort has been made to faithfully reproduce the original booklets, hence the scanning of the original covers and photos. With the kind permission of James' family.

Reading through these books written more than 30 years ago, I'm struck by just how much James got right. He wrote at a time of the salmonella scares, yet this was to be replaced over the years by SARS, vCJD mad cow, and all the way through to Covid-19. And every one of these diseases has originated from humans eating animals.

Gandhi called it "the blackest of all crimes" and James frequently refers to the wholly immoral practice of vivisection. Home Office figures released 4th July 2022 show that 3.06 million live animals were experimented upon in the UK in 2021, a 6% increase on the previous year. Worldwide, the figure is some 115 million, which equates to around 450 innocent and defenceless lives lost in the time taken to read this foreword.

Some will think James' views on the subject as unfounded rhetoric, but as someone who has worked in two laboratories, I can endorse all he has said. The Lethal Dose 50 test that James refers to, is still the mainstay of the industry and one has to sign at induction that one understands this. I well remember one Christmas Eve and speaking to a scientist who was uneasy at killing off a large batch of rodents that hadn't been experimented upon. The reason: while we humans were celebrating Christmas and New Year, the creatures would have put on weight and become invalid for the experiment (cocaine in this instance, with probes inserted into their heads to measure brain reactions). There's no such thing as a happy Christmas, or any other day, for the very many species of animal inside a laboratory.

I assure the reader of twenty-eight horses being killed by exsanguination in another experiment. They had ended up in a laboratory was because they were some of the many that don't make money for the callous horse racing industry. Discarded as rubbish, like the betting slips on the bookmaker's floor that condemned them.

Every creature in the lab is a sentient being with a personality – no different whatsoever to our beloved family pets that we would never put through this torture and death. But we still mostly look away from the laboratories and slaughterhouses, out of sight and out of mind.

James was a good friend to many, and brought humanitarian comfort and kindness to thousands over his clerical lifetime; he was the hospital chaplain in Aberdeen at the time of the Piper Alpha disaster. His compassion for all creation shines through in these booklets and I hope his message will linger long within us.

To see James on his TV appearances over the years, please visit: youtube.com/user/bigbaba5b/videos

My thanks to Jennie and Paul Zehler, and to Jill Copeland and Adrian Yardley, for their help and encouragement in compiling this new volume. However, the biggest thanks of all goes to James Thompson; his life and courageous work has been an inspiration and blessing to so many who knew him. I hope his relentless endeavour to challenge and change Christian doctrine and dogma will never be forgotten. His resting place at Brynford Pet Cemetery says it all:

> **Revd. James Thompson**
> *"The Animals' Padre"*
> 4. 2. 1930 - 30. 1. 2015
> *His Love and Compassion*
> *Embraced the Whole of Creation*

Phillip Jones
September 2022

Contents

Retreat From Responsibility (1989) 1

Cast Out of The Ark (1994).. 17

A Cleric's Contempt of Animal-based Cancer Research (1990).... 101

Reflections of a Spiritual Tramp (1996) 119

Praise for Creatures Great and Small (1988) 157

Other books by James Thompson:
The Bible, The Church & The Animal Kingdom (1989)
How to Bounce Through Life (1996)
The Young Spiritual Tramp (2005)

'Prayer Of A Laboratory Animal'

Creator of the sky and sea;
Of tiger, monkey, fish and bee.
Lord God of all that lives I dare;
To offer up my humble prayer.
I've woken from my fitful sleep,
With heavy heart and sorrow deep.
I dreamed of days when I was free,
And played and gambolled in the trees.

Alone imprisoned in this cage,
I try to calm my fear and rage.
How can I face another day
Of being tortured in this way?
Soon they'll come for me again,
And take me to their place of pain.
Please tell me Lord for I don't know,
Why do these people hate me so?

They've cut my vocal cords and tied
A heavy bandage round my eyes
I cannot see, I cannot scream,
This all seems like a fearful dream.
Twas yesterday that day of dread,
They took my friend, and now he's dead.
I tremble Lord, it's plain to see,
Today the victim will be me.

I hear their footsteps coming near,
O Lord my heart is full of fear.
I need you more than I can tell,
To free me from this earthy hell.
Great God who brought the world to birth,
And all the creatures of the earth.
Who made the stars, the moon, the sun,
Please let me die before they come.

Acknowledgement to ANN SIMS

'RETREAT' FROM RESPONSIBILITY
CHRISTIAN APATHY and the ANIMAL CAUSE

by Revd James Thompson,

Further copies available from St Clement's Publications:
at 39p.

ALSO:

'PRAISE FOR CREATURES GREAT & SMALL' - the Pet Lovers
Hymnal, at £2.28.   Music Supplement: 90p.

'THE BIBLE, THE CHURCH & THE ANIMAL KINGDOM' - an
indictment of Christendom by Revd James Thompson (Due
out September 1989), at £2.49.

and all prices include p&p!

Introduction

Almost two thousand years ago Jesus of Nazareth was crucified, and those who were responsible for His crucifixion were the religious leaders of the time. He had denounced them for their hypocrisy because they implied that God was solely concerned about them and no-one else outside their race – those who were outside of Judaism were accursed of God (John 7:49).

These scribes and Pharisees of Jesus' time limited the benevolence, love and compassion of God as exclusive to their own race. But these first century religious hypocrites actually did even worse than that, they perverted and distorted moral issues. Our Saviour inferred that, morally speaking, they magnified gnats as they swallowed camels whole (Matthew 23:24)! One was allowed to exploit Gentiles left right and centre, but if one ate with hands not washed then one was classed as profane; a ceremonial law had been broken (Mark 7:5). Well, that's purely by way of introduction!

I use the above analogy because I'm convinced that if Jesus visibly ministered in a manner similar to two thousand years ago then the modern counterparts of those first century scribes and Pharisees: many pontiffs, prelates and priests, would be the first to get rid of Him. And this because Jesus would surely denounce most of them for the same kind of reasons – limiting the mercy, love and compassion of Almighty God, and putting moral priorities completely out of perspective.

As a priest of the worldwide Anglican communion, I openly accuse each one of its branches of falsely betraying the love, mercy and compassion of

God by making them far too small. Indeed, to the leaders of each major denominations I would equally say: 'You take the God of the Bible and by your theology you shrink Him and His love as only embracing humanity! The God of my Bible made room for the animals within the ark (Genesis 7:14), but you exclude them from your ark of salvation. My God is concerned about the beasts of the field and the birds of the air (Psalm 50:10-11), where you have limited His love and all-embracing compassion to your own motley species.'

Now you may well ask: "How has this appalling state of affairs come about? When did all the rot set in?" Well, the culprit is post biblical theology and it was severely corrupted in western Christendom by a supposedly angelic teacher of the Latin stream! His name was Thomas Aquinas, who was to go so far as to dogmatically affirm that animals have no souls; and on this earth can have no rights whatsoever! And Thomas's became THE philosophy of his church. As a recent consequence, even this very year (1989), a catholic archbishop hits the headlines in many newspapers throughout the civilised world by stating 'It's not a sin to beat a dog!' And amazingly, regardless of all the criticism levelled against him Archbishop Battisi still stands by what he has affirmed! Yes, I'm convinced that the darkest period within those Dark Ages was through the Roman church accepting Aquinas's teaching as the official theology of their church. For it was then that Catholicism rejected the teachings of the saintly Francis of Assisi in preference for the dogmatism of their 'so-called' angelic doctor.

Lest you feel, however, that I am slanted solely against Rome in its lack of concern for animals I wish to make it clear that this is not so. Much of its theology was unconsciously carried over by the reformers into their denominations. I attended an evangelical renewal meeting, a year or so ago, within the Church of England. During a question time there, when I suggested that there surely could be no true manifestation of God in a church which excluded animals, I was howled to derision by several clergy: "What connection can there possibly be between animal concern and the Holy Spirit?" they asked, and then one or two just about burst their sides before waiting for an answer.

Spurious Sanctification!

So lacking in vital moral issues has Christendom become, that it's not been unknown to tuck into veal at a religious retreat, or crack open battery eggs; while during the meal a monk, nun or spiritual director reads an extract some devotional work, if not the Bible itself – exemplifying the life of 'holiness'. Yes, more often than not the latter word is interpreted as having no broader a connotation than a quality associated with low voices, robes, cloisters, solemnity, rituals, or archaic and musty buildings! Yes, it's an interpretation of holiness quite different to that expressed by the Baptists and Elijahs of the good book (Matthew 11:7-15), not to mention the Nazarene Himself!

If you think I'm speaking 'out of my hat' then let me tell you of a convent in Davenport, the where up to a few months ago, despite repeated protests by reputable animal rightists, the nuns - who were encircled by acres of open land – when not engaged in regular prayer and worship ran a highly lucrative 'battery farm'. Animal welfare campaigners, with absolute justification, termed their particular establishment an 'animal Belsen' where hens were over crammed in filthy cages and deprived of all exercise. Thankfully, due to constant protests from, it might appear, all but the 'religious!', their vile trade has now terminated. As indeed, so has the appalling veal farm of the monks at Storrington priory. Monks and nuns, however, are not alone in their callous and often appallingly cruel abuse of animals. Abroad – particularly in the Latin countries – the barbarity that is often associated with church festivals has to be seen to be believed. But then way back in the last century, when a society for the protection of animals was about to be established in Rome itself it was the Pope who intervened and stopped it. "It would imply that humans had duties towards animals!", he said. Yes, and did not the Good Shepherd say, 'By their fruits you shall know them!"

One senses that if the scribes and pharisees picked out (moral) gnats while swallowing camels, then they didn't do it half as well as many so-called Christian leaders do it today. But then, perhaps it's expecting too much to assume that a humanely prepared dish akin to vegetarianism, would be acceptable to those who live in palaces – and that's where leading prelates often live! I suppose the inconsistency appears more relevant when one considers the austerity and moral strictures associated with a monastery or a convent. Indeed, there these religious communities will speak up about: there is the four lettered word; the non-attendance at mass; the taking of a pill or wearing of a Durex (depending on which sex); and the neglect of saying stereotyped prayers morning and night. Indeed, without a list of such sins there would be no need of a spiritual director or a father confessor!

There are the assumed crucial subjects of woman's place in the Church, as well as what liturgy should be followed. And all these things may well be discussed with much heated emotion. Yes, after one has indulged in, and enjoyed without a qualm of conscience, the products of animal Belsens!

Sin as classed by Holy Church!

During the less organised or free periods, while enjoying a church retreat from this world (when one thinks individually without being conditioned collectively!), topics as diverse as a bullfight in Spain or a vivisection lab in Aberdeen might well be touched upon – not, of course, out of compassion for the animals; holy church has agreed that they have no rights as such; but possibly because the former is a pastime enjoyable to man's leisure periods abroad – many clerics included! And the latter is deemed to, somehow, benefit the life span of humanity upon earth! Of course, a whole host of other subjects could similarly be included for a light period of discussion either within the common room or while walking through the serene, tranquil grounds outside. I merely single these two subjects out as both of them have the official backing of holy church. Pope Paul VI having warmly welcomed and given a private audience to an official group of bullfighters in 1972, at which he gave them his special blessing. And the same leader of Christendom having officially endorsed the practice of vivisection previously in 1966!

Now, admittedly, vivisectors as well as bullfighters are only human. They are liable to commit sins. These, however, could never be enacted against an animal, says holy church. As already mentioned, animals are not considered persons so they are conveniently excluded! But just in case even a vivisector should fall in to 'top degree' sin – for example, missing mass on a Sunday or holy day of obligation; or, if a female – taking the pill, then, holy church has sought during their employment hours to meet such needs: chapels with a confessional available are occasionally attached to centres for animal experimentation! Respectable Aberdeen's Marischal college in which vivisection (the blackest of all crimes: to quote Mahatma Gandhi!) takes place, has a place of worship dedicated to the followers of St Francis outwardly attached to it: the Presbyterian Parish Church of Greyfriars!

Exclusive Piety!

Yes, this strange exclusion of the animal kingdom from the church's prayer, praise and worship; and its worse side, the callous and often cruel ill treatment of sub human life by those who call themselves followers of the Good Shepherd, is quite an enigma. It has corrupted every tradition of Christendom. No branch is immune. I'll give you just one more instance from many; that of a Yorkshire farmer of two decades previous. The man was a modern-day Puritan as well as a gifted Methodist lay preacher. He considered his religion a duty, and he was as straight in his dealings, it would appear, as a die. The man was a strict teetotaller referring to alcohol as the devil's own brew! During the age of the mini skirt, he frequently frowned upon it as pandering to the lusts of the flesh. Indeed, so staunch was he to his beliefs that when a certain employee uttered a profanity the man was warned that if it ever happened again then instant dismissal would follow. Yes, and this fiery twentieth century Puritan would have stood by every word he said.

Alas, the above paragraph refers to only one side of the farmer in question. I was later able to enter his farm premises, and what I saw there quite horrified me: calves tethered in stalls where they couldn't even turn sideways; where they were kept in semi darkness, and no doubt fed on an iron deficient diet so as to whiten their flesh for the gourmets.

Pigs were tethered in iron maidens resulting in bleeding nipples. And hens were crammed in animal Belsens for speeded egg production. How could he do such things? How could he be so callous? Well, if I'd have called him a hypocrite then he would have been quite taken back. It's the last thing he would have considered himself to be! Yes, as I see it, he was just the outcome of a religious conditioning which is a distortion of the biblical revelation.

Light from the word of God

'Whoso would be a man must be a nonconformist'. wrote Emerson. But leaders within Christendom are hardly likely to agree. Most of them have climbed the hierarchic ladder through conforming to the theology of their respective denominations. Few of them are desirous, or even capable, of throwing off past traditions so as to get back to the blessed Bible. They, as a group, only approach the sacred volume either in the light of the Latin fathers or else in the light of the Puritan reformers. Would to God that they might allow the book of books to be its own interpreter with the sole assistance of the Holy Spirit! For then – and only then – will they discover that God is a far greater God than they've ever understood. And within it they will find an order of moral priorities vastly different to their own. Oh yes, they will certainly find that the volume written for man puts man in proper perspective. They will learn of how man was made in God's image before he fell from grace (Genesis 1:27). And they will also discover that God's character is divinely expressed in the analogy of a herdsman's care of the animals entrusted to his charge: 'The Lord is my shepherd' (Psalm 23:1). Well, what a tribute to the character of nomadic shepherds of a far-off age! No wonder angels appeared to THEM to tell of the birth of One who would call Himself the Good Shepherd (Luke 2:9)!

Now I don't know about your Bible but mine tells me a great deal about God's concern for the animal kingdom! He made more than one covenant with it (Genesis 9:10 & Hosea 2:18): and He tells me in no uncertain terms that a righteous man will care for his beast (Proverbs 12:10). And I also learn that beasts can have a spiritual perception which supposedly God-fearing humans can lack (Numbers 22:27). I learn that animals can not only perceive the spiritual, but be very much influenced by it (Luke 19:30&35). I learn that an extra bird thrown in by man as worthless is of value to The Lord (compare Matthew 10:29 with Luke 12:6-71). And I learn that when Eden is more than restored then vegetarianism will be the norm instead of the exception (Isaiah 11:6-9). But until that blessed age of peace is established, I know that the whole of creation groans in travail; waiting – so longingly and expectantly – for the sons and daughters of God to manifest their characters through bringing about their liberation (Romans 8:19). Alas, how much longer must the dumb creation wait? How much longer are 'born again' Christians going to shirk their responsibility in being a mouthpiece for the defenceless of God's creation? I don't like to say this, but I sincerely feel that far too many Christians are so heavenly minded as to be no earthly good for God. Brothers and sisters in Christ, these things should not be!

I can't answer for you, dear reader, but I'm grateful myself that though there are more animals and insects in this world than there are humans, God made me one of the latter! Bearing this in mind, and realising that someday I will be called to give account of my stewardship. What will I be able to say to the One who not only called Himself the Good Shepherd but was also pleased to be referred to in terms of an animal: a lion as well as a lamb (Revelation 5:5 & 22:1)? There IS a place for man's dominion over the creation, but let us never forget that it implies that of a caring master, and not that of a tyrant or a despot. Alas, the latter categories are akin to the inhumane way that man treats defenceless animals today. And it has a close affinity with the way whites treated blacks a mere century or two earlier. And, was not the reason given very much the same? Yes, isolated biblical verses were wrenched from context to justify it; the creatures reared in captivity were said to have known no other form of life. And perhaps most important of all, it was condoned as being an economic necessity!

Sowing and Reaping!

It is my honest contention that we need Wilberforces for the battle against animal slavery. But I realise that the opposition comes from similar if not identical sources: mercenary minded tycoons, pathetic prelates, and one or two who quote out of context an isolated verse or two of Scripture so as to perpetuate evil. Well, be that as it may I know that what one sows one will inevitably reap (Galatians 6:7), and that though we reap to the wind we'll reap a whirlwind (Hosea 8:7)! Factors as diverse as the colour problem, the scourge of AIDS and a recent national salmonella egg scare, are but a backlash from past evil. There is also some reasonable evidence to support a theory that the AIDS virus came from a vivisection lab; just as there is that the salmonella egg contamination was linked with battery conditions in which the poor creatures are forced to eat pellets containing their own excrement if not the carcasses of fellow creatures.

Friend, once a nation cultivates callousness it soon condones cruelty. And the latter does not usually stop with perpetrating evil towards defenceless animals, it moves on to defenceless humans too. Cruelty to animals usually precedes cruelty to children, and this paves the way for cruelty towards adults. And then when the latter seek to defend themselves the outcome is abominable warfare with all its related evils.

If we torture the defenceless then not only will it come back in boomerang effect, possibly in a way we had not envisaged, but it is my contention that we'll corrupt ourselves in the process. Let me try and illustrate my point: I spent a couple of years in Ulster many moons ago – I haven't lost the accent I then picked up! You wonder why terrorists there can blow up innocent folk there without a qualm of conscience or remorse? Well, I'll tell you where it started – back at church schools the young were frequently indoctrinated to believe that God was concerned about their church alone. The other side were either heretics or else idolaters depending on whether you were catholic or protestant. Then, similarly, in the biology class one was bullied out of being squeamish; 'they're only beasts on the slab, God hasn't given them a soul!' Yes, the process of exclusion from compassion – a hardening process – evolves until one is completely desensitised to compassion outside one's own 'elect' circle. And when this succeeds then it opens wide the gate for sadism of the most depraved kind. Do not forget for one moment that the fictitious Dr Jekyll as well as the factual Doctor Mengele were both vivisectors!

Reader, if only in decades past the two western Christian traditions had put their emphasis on the example of the Good Shepherd or that of good St Francis! This world would then have become a better place for all forms of life; and as for trouble spots such as dear Ulster, why it would have become a Beulah rather than a blood bath!

Conclusion:

'What is God really like?' asked the enquirer of far-off Bible times. 'Just look at the way a herdsman cares for members of another species', was the teaching of the Psalmist. 'To that very extent the God of Israel cares for you. There you have the answer!

'The Lord is my shepherd, so I'll not want' replies the Israelite. What a compliment to those herdsmen of old! But what a dawning indictment on the impersonal intensive husbandry which is the legacy of Christendom today! To use the example of an intensive factory farm breeder as an analogy of God's dealings with us would be to transform the Deity into the very devil himself!

Next time YOU go on a retreat. Why not take the Bible and a concordance as your sole books of devotion! Be no longer blinded by the theologian who loves to blur the pure water of the Word of God through terms of analysis and formulas of H2O. Look for each reference to animals within the sacred pages. See them in the light of the Good Shepherd's character, concern and care. Remember that He – and not the conflicting theologians – is the key to Scriptures as well as the door into the Father's sheepfold. Who knows, you might even find a Creator and a Redeemer whose compassion and concern is for the ultimate restoration of all living things!

Then I heard every creature in heaven and on earth and under the earth and on the sea, and all that is in them, singing:

"To HIM who sits on the throne and to the LAMB be praise and honour and glory and power, for ever and ever!"

A PRAYER:

Glorious Christ whose analogy was that of a Good Shepherd, make us more like Yourself, so that we may express towards the dumb creation as much compassion and care as did humble shepherds who lived before you died.

Shame us from our lack of sensitivity and care. Teach us who boast of Calvary to know that we are not the whole of the world for which you suffered. Take the blindness from our eyes, the predjudice from our minds and the haughtiness from our hearts.

Save us from the arrogance which makes your love far too small, confining it to our own species, just as your children once confined it to their own race.

Make us aware of the fact that what mankind sows it will inevitably reap, for we are all interdependent upon each other and your moral laws can never be traversed with impunity.

Lord grant that even the air which surrounds us may give out from us vibrations of love and trust, so that all animals will recognise in us the manifestation of your children.

Lord, accept this prayer, and make us all kind under shepherds. We ask this for Your Name's sake.

AMEN

39p

St Clement's Publications
14 Cluny Square
BUCKIE, Banffshire
Scotland
AB5 1HA
Tel (0542) 32312

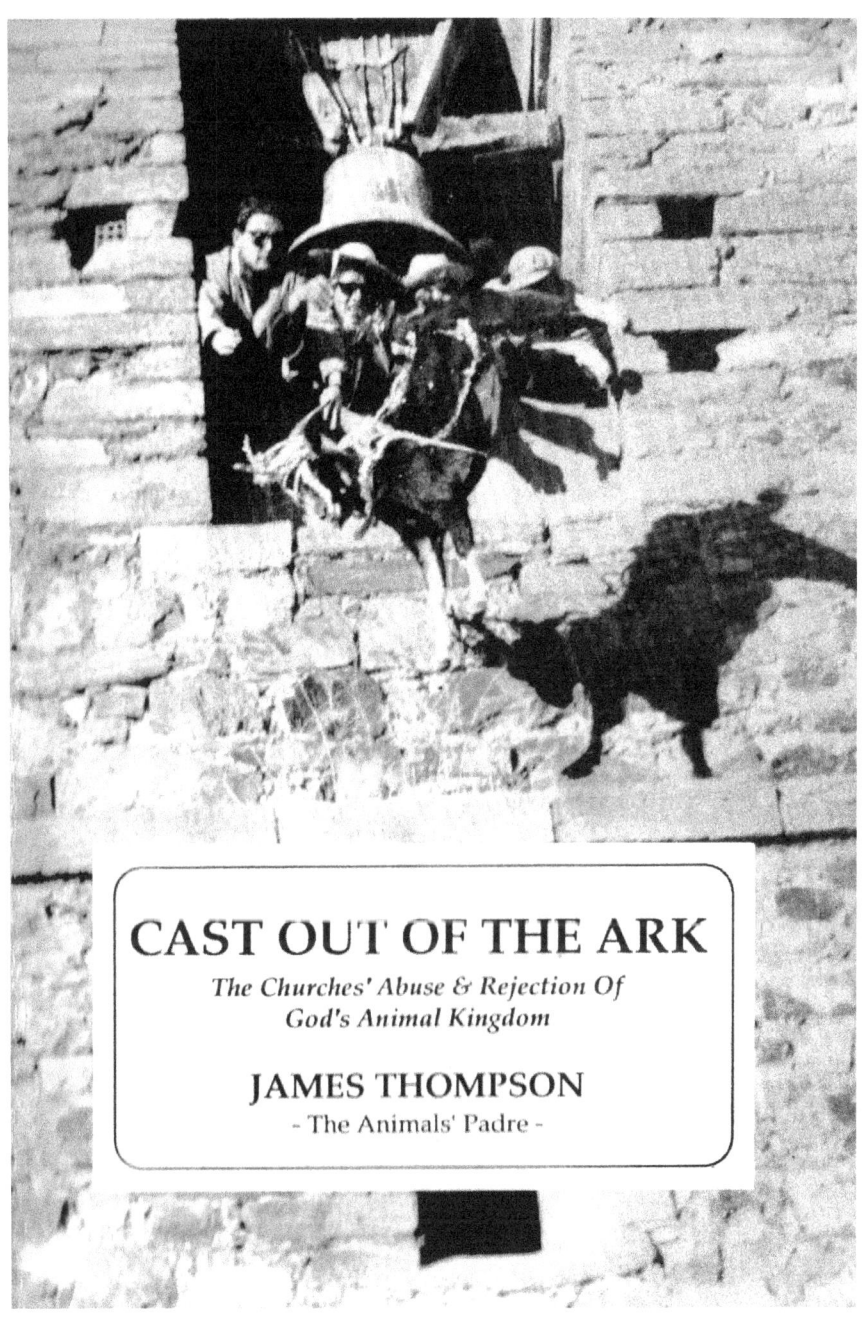

CAST OUT OF THE ARK
The Churches' Abuse & Rejection Of God's Animal Kingdom

JAMES THOMPSON
- The Animals' Padre -

CAST OUT OF THE ARK

Christendom's appalling abuse of God's animal creation

By

The Rev. James Thompson

Acknowledgement: The author is most grateful to Gillian Russell for her helpful advice; to Tony and Vicky Moore for front cover photograph and those of Spain inside; and to his dedicated wife, Doreen, for her typesetting.

ISBN 0 9523022 0 9
© 1994 James Thompson
TY COCH PUBLISHING
14 Cluny Square
Moray AB56 1HA

'We Christians talk a lot about holy living; sometimes about being 'baptised in the spirit'. However, our TRUE spiritual depth is mirrored for all to see. It's in the way we treat God's helpless!'

The Author.

Prologue

This book was written with our nation's majority in view – those who would wish to be termed 'Animal Loving Britons'. Of this majority the greater number would still wish to retain the name of Christian. This is not to imply that they are weekly worshippers at a local church or chapel but it does imply that they were, mostly, christened as infants, prefer to marry in church, and will expect a cleric to offer prayers at their demise.

For most people, being termed Christian is basically to live by the golden rule which Jesus taught and also exemplified. Unfortunately, most of these people, if pressed, would have to admit that they really know little more idea concerning what He did! An apt summary of sense: to be nice to all types, to refuse to rock the boat, - a laissez faire attitude of 'live and let live' an attitude of 'don't poke your nose where it's not wanted!' and a desire to see the good while closing one's eyes to the bad.

Thankfully, there are many in society today who are no longer satisfied with the above superficial interpretation. These people want to find out from the very source what Christianity is all about. Some such people will seek an answer through pursuing an introductory course given by one of the many denominations. They might accept such a one as 'What the Catholic church teaches'. They might equally find a divergent approach through one of several evangelical channels: 'How to be Born Again' might be one of many titles. Equally, the fringe movements (referred to by the 'once' major denominations as the sects) are also keen to offer their own neatly packaged Bible studies as to what Christianity is all about.

The remarkable fact is that each of the above exponents of the Faith will give a unique interpretation, but as all these Movements accept the teachings of the Old and New Testaments as a basic foundation, we shall be wise to go to this fountain-head to search these Scriptures for ourselves to find out how Biblically accurate and consistent these Movements are with them. The early Christians at Berea were congratulated by St Paul for doing this very thing. (Acts 17:11) You, the reader, will equally be wise to go to the original source to find out what Jesus taught, the very religion in which He was cradled and the kind of example He set forth.

In doing the above you will learn that the teaching and example of

Jesus is sometimes as far removed from current denominational practice as the moon is from cheese! Let two instances suffice: consider the titles, trimmings and trappings of top ecclesiastical dignitaries and consider the way they pray. Then read Jesus' attitude towards it all in Matthew 23:1-12 and Matthew 6:7-18!

With the exception of some Unitarians and Quakers, our country's major denominations believe that Jesus was more than a teacher sent from God. They affirm He was no less than the Creator, made visible in human flesh. The deduction then is that the more in keeping your morality is with the teaching and example of Jesus, then the more Christ-like you have become. Indeed, literally, the more godly you are!

Historically, it is highly credible that Jesus of Nazareth, whom we call God's 'anointed one' (Messiah in Hebrew and 'Christ' in Greek) began His ministry when he was round thirty years of age. That this lasted a mere two and a half years and that this was so revolutionary as to change the whole history of the world, we testify to, every time we write the date! This is all the more remarkable when one considers that Jesus was humanly a child of poverty and void of college education, and this Jesus entrusted His whole manifesto to a motley, mixed group – excepting, possibly, the more refined Judas.

Yet no earthly emperor nor dictator (and not even the combined armies of the world) has done so much for western humanity as this one solitary figure from the backwoods of first century Palestine: Jesus from Nazareth of Galilee (John 1:46). It was truly said, 'No man spake as He. (John 7:46)! He never compromised the truth, in fact He claimed to be the very truth itself. Though such a claim coming from anyone else would have sounded preposterous and blasphemous, coming from Jesus, it didn't.

You see, to most, Christ's marvellous works were a seal to the veracity of His claims, the natural outcome of an unsurpassed ethical life. Of course, you don't have to believe these miracle accounts, yet the marvellous thing is that they cease to appear as mere accretions once one has experienced Him in life.

In a very real sense, many believe in Jesus, not so much because of the life He lived, but for the life He helps them to live? To those of us who follow, He seems always in front; and to those who are the champions of the exploited and oppressed, He is very much at their side. It was Lincoln who said, "I never found Christ so near as when I stooped down to break the chains from the feet of the slaves. I then felt, as it were, the very hand of Christ upon my shoulder." This is reminiscent of Schweitzer's memorable words:

> *'He comes to us as One unknown, without a name, as of old by the lake-side. He came to those who knew Him not. He speaks to us the same word. 'Follow thou Me,' and sets us to the task which He has to fulfil for our time. He commands. And to those who obey Him, whether they be wise or simple, He will reveal Himself in the toils, the conflicts, the sufferings which they shall pass through in His fellowship, and, as an ineffable mystery, they shall learn in their own experience who He is.'*

Bearing the above quotations in mind, we realise that there is an evil in our midst as heinous as any human slave trade. It exists before our very eyes today, hence the purpose of this publication. **To those who fight against this Satanic force, I would say: "Take heart, Christ's hand is upon your shoulder!' 'He is not dead but very much alive – as you'll discover when you obey the call of your conscience. The fight is His as well as yours." The opposition may be intense, but one with Christ is always a majority!** Human corruption has hardly changed within two thousand years. Those who take up a prophet's role and become troublers of national life, as Elijah became a 'troubler of Israel', must expect the wrath of the descendants of the priests of Baal.

The Founder of Christianity was thought by many of His day to be Elijah returned. It so happened that people were not opposed to reincarnation as is so in most Christian circles! Jesus, while indirectly referring to it (Matthew 17:10-13), never took occasion to denounce it (John 9:2 and Matthew 16:13-14)! However, all this is purely incidental to our theme. The real issue is that Jesus was not a sloppy, spineless, sentimental softie but, on the contrary, an agitator, a reformer and a revolutionary on behalf of the exploited – just as Elijah had been. Consequently, if anyone deserved a wooden spoon, Jesus did. Indeed, one of the charges brought against Him was that He was 'a stirrer of the people' (Luke 23:5)!

Those who follow Jesus should become stirrers too, lest they prove unworthy to bear His name. How many of us are prepared to pay such a price? Neutral we cannot remain! Like Him, we should combine within our nature a dual character exemplified in two beasts: the lion and the lamb. He was referred to in Scripture as 'The Lion of the tribe of Judah' (Revelation 5:5) and also as 'The Lamb of God' (John 1:29)! It is necessary that we also utilise and harmonise such contrasting traits – as will prove apparent as one reads on.

Stirrers and Revolutionaries have always been 'up against it' once their aims conflicted with the pleasures and purses of the ruling rich. It was so with the Old Testament prophets: it was so with Our Lord Himself: it was so with the apostles, the martyrs and reformers. Human nature is no different today. The humble folk hear Jesus gladly – and He warned them to beware of the religious elite (Mark 12:37 & 38). The latter preferred to fraternise with the world's powerful than stick their necks out for the oppressed. Sticking out one's neck is often asking for it to be chopped off, and only those with the character and calibre of a John the Baptist will do it. John wasn't so much bothered about his head, for God had secured his heart! Make sure God has won your heart, for only then will you surrender your life for His cause.

"But why expect the above kind of clash?" one might ask. Sufficient to say that vast religious systems, having made themselves secure through fraternising with the rich and wealthy of this world, find it increasingly difficult to offend those who offer them hospitality, support and status. The trinkets and refinery of the Manor House are much more acceptable to the social climbing cleric than the chipped beaker and bun at the workman's cottage! And if hunting and furs go with the former, who but an ungrateful wretch is likely to condemn the pastimes of those who pour out from the gin bottle, send round a brace of pheasants to the Rectory, and slip into the hand a handsome cheque at the festive season? The writer is relating to his own experience!

Present concern for Animal reform has much in common with a previous concern to abolish slavery; and it is a dreadful blot on the Church of England to reflect that some of Wilberforce's most active opponents were within the House of Bishops. It would appear the hobnobbing had got many of the latter their gaiters! Subsequently, it proved more expedient and less expensive to denounce Wilberforce than lose face with Gentry having vested interest in the slave trade.

Bishops of the past are not of course alone in deserving castigation: Victorian vicars, and chapel ministers too, were more often than not little better! It is interesting to find that though Victorian preachers – especially those in Nonconformity – were obsessed with the evils of alcohol, indolence and theft (all factors counter-productive to industry!); there was at the same time a remarkable silence from their pulpits concerning the much greater evils that prevailed. Tied houses, long working hours, poor pay and filthy factory conditions, were factors considered irrelevant for pulpit oratory. Children would be mercilessly thrashed for indolence, as well as tied to looms to stop them wandering; and such factors were morally acceptable, yet should these poor wretches utter a blasphemy then the isolated utterance alone would be deemed evil and worth of clerical ostracism.

Popular preachers of Victorian and Edwardian nonconformity knew how to manufacture the right kind of rhetoric and emotion: plenty of fervour and steam in a direction truly pleasing to the ruling classes who were often pillars and bastions of religious respectability. Consequently, to fight for the exploited mill hand who was unable to fend for himself, was hardly the aspiration of clerics who (often coming up from a lower social rank) loved their new found prestige for themselves and their family, hobnobbing with the mill owner and his family, or the aristocratic board of directors – who were frequently the deacons on a Sunday!

Yes, the hypocrisy of a morality, which claimed to be Christian while in practice it actually opposed most of what Christ taught and did, was the fruit of an apostate and faithless Christendom. It was a blasphemous distortion of the Jesus of history, and alas, it is the present writer's conviction that such hypocrisy is rampant today!

The whole of Christendom stands guilty before God; and this is largely because of the Church's proven inability to study the Scriptures without being influenced by post biblical tradition – and reading the latter to the former. Indeed, to approach the Bible without preconceived theological moulds, will result in the perception of not only a moral evolvement but also an inclusiveness of which the animal creation is a very real and integral part. As it is, the influence of Latin Scholasticism has polluted more than a single branch of Christendom; it has indirectly contaminated the whole tree.

Oh that people approaching the sacred volume of Holy Scripture would allow it to speak for itself! For they will then be able to appreciate the many relevant passages concerning animals; as well, of course, as the moral need for right priorities at all times. Only then, will they be able to perceive a retrograde process within Christendom which has culminated in so many reprehensible practices against the animal creation. And it is the present writer's contention that these latter bring their own retributive penalties upon us. Thankfully – and not before time – we are witnessing more and more reactionary protests.

This concise volume then touches very briefly on the existence of humane remedies procurable for the ills of mankind before culminating with a list of biblical references producible to substantiate – and even further – the Creator's concern for bird and beast.

Relevant Passages

The world of the biblical era is far more inclusive and spiritually embracing than the puny anthropocentric world of Christendom. It is in many respects a very tonic for the Christian animal lover to behold. It reveals a God whose dealings are not only with humanity but with the larger creation with which He showed concern by providing room for them within the Ark (Genesis 7:8). Later He showed equal concern for them in the story of Jonah (Jonah 3:8 & 8:11)!

Speaking as the human mouth piece for God the psalmist says, "All the beasts of the forest are mine; and so are the cattle of a thousand hills. I know all the fowls upon the mountains; and the wild beasts of the field are in my sight!" (Psalm 50:10-11). Yes, and these creatures know God! (Job 12:7-9). The birds and beasts were viewed upon as 'believers' (Job 38:41, Joel 1:20, Psalm 104:21) - along with the living creation (Psalm 145:15). Atheism in those far off biblical times was only attributable to the foolish of humanity (Psalm 14:1).

God still speaks today through beasts of burden perceptive to angelic presences, while men who abuse them are spiritually blind - just as was the case in the time of Balaam (Numbers 32:22). Indeed, the conversation is still no doubt two-fold as animals are not as dumb as haughty humans would like to affirm. An Iris Hughes summed it so well for us in her anthology, IN THE ARK:

> 'Animals have their own way of talking to those who will take the trouble to learn their language. Animals speak with their eyes and a sensitive person finds it very hard to resist the pleading in the eyes of many animals. Then they have vocal sounds which mean a lot to those who know the language. They are certainly not dumb, as is so often said. They also talk with body movements, as in the case of a tail-wagging dog, or a cat affectionately rubbing one's legs asking for food. So, if we just take a little trouble, we may learn a lot.'

An example comes vividly to mind concerning a retired miner who once confessed to the writer of how he had so lost his temper as to punch a pit pony in the face because that particular day, at the commencement of the shift, the stubborn animal refused to budge. He said that when he saw a little blood trickle from its nose, he felt a real twinge of conscience. "The look in that creature's eyes filled me with remorse", he said.

Indeed, he felt worse later! Because the seam the creature refused to enter that day became, a few moments later, the scene of a horrific roof fall! Subsequently, Mr West (for that was his name) swore that the pony had received a premonition which saved their lives. That retired miner became the writer's earliest supporter in the cause against animal abuse.

When the writer, as a Doncaster curate, exposed the cruelty of young thugs for having strangled a cat from a branch in a nearby wood, the press were anxious to publish the story. When a month or two later more thugs were criticised by him for using air guns at birds the publicity increased. Soon the curate's vicar was 'up in arms' because young people in the parish were being shown up for their barbarism! The mothers of these vandals were being consoled by their vicar who was strongly opposed to this curate's militance. Indeed, the latter owes a debt of gratitude to that gentleman of the colliery who, twenty-five years ago, stood faithfully at his side.

The wisest of all men stated how a just person will care for his beast (Proverbs 12:10). Truly, how frightfully ungodly mankind has become! In the ark of the Twentieth Century Church there should be as much a place allotted to the animals as there was in Noah's. Indeed, His Covenant after the flood was directed as much to them as it was to man! (Genesis 8:10). But alas, mention their inclusion today within worship and you could well end up with either deacons or diocese coming down upon you like a ton of bricks: 'sacrilege!" might well be the cry. Yes, we are far, far removed from the ethos of Biblical times!

Life is not as God first willed (Genesis 1:31). Through the consequence of Adam's fall, the defenceless are exploited, and sin spreads resulting in ruin, degradation and death. The results of global disruption reverberate throughout creation, and this is expressed throughout Scripture, if not factually then certainly mythically. The larger creation longs and yearns for deliverance – through the intervention of spiritually awakened Christians – from this bondage that prevails. St Paul (no sentimentalist of animals) touched on this very theme in Romans 8:19.

I ask, how much longer must this sad fallen world wait before the sons of God are morally motivated to prepare for Paradise or make a path for the Millennium? Some are wrapped up with equating the Holy Spirit with nice feelings for themselves that they're little better than drug addicts living in euphoria, unconcerned with sadism and greed that surrounds them. However, the Scriptures infer that there will become a time when the Paradise that was lost by the first Adam will be restored by the second Adam – Christ. But how far most Christians will have worked to actualise it, will be a quite different matter!

We pray, 'Thy kingdom come. Thy will be done on earth'; and we sing about it too; but, as a presence in the world we've shirked being His mystical body. Looking closer into Genesis it would seem that in Paradise animals, though under the dominion of man, were as free as was woman under the dominion of her husband! It would imply that in Eden there was order and graded authority to be equated with the later guardianship and Biblical form of a faithful stewardship, far removed from any exploitation and oppression.

Animals along with their human neighbours were vegetarian in diet (Genesis 1:28-30). Permission to become carnivorous was only given to man after the flood, preceded by a prediction of animal fear towards a fallen humanity (Genesis 9:2). Nevertheless, this temporal era of sin will ultimately be overthrown by a Paradise Restored, and once again, vegetarianism will become universal (Isaiah 11:7).

Isaiah's idyllic vision of this future Paradise – or as some would term it, Millennium reign, - surely gladdens the heart of every animal lover! Such language is much more than the expression of poetic imagery, and it is supportive of that much later Pauline teaching concerning the final restoration of all things (Ephesians 1:10) What is more, it has its crescendo within the last great volume of Holy Scripture: the figurative book of Revelation.

Here, we have an apocalyptic vision, and in it we see beasts as well as humans worshipping before the very throne of God itself. And here, wonder of wonders. It is the animals which take precedence in worship over human elders (Revelation 5:5) and as a land (Revelation 5:6-8). A vast contrast from today, when thanks to church conditioning, to call a human 'a beast' is to insult him.

Also, within this last book of the sacred volume – and mindful of the covenant that was given to beasts as well as humans in the first – the rainbow appears above the very throne of God as, after the flood, it had appeared in the sky. Yes, both books have much in common, and as one of them figuratively expresses the Divine commencement the other figuratively expresses the Divine consummation. But, between what one might aptly term 'Paradise Lost' and 'Paradise Regained' there is the whole gambit of earthly history which is so relevant to us – for we are a part of it!

What else has God to say from Scripture, relevant to the animal creation? The answer is 'a great deal indeed!' First of all, whether we like it or not, throughout the Old Testament era as well as the beginning of the New, animals were sacrificed in worship, and that at great expense. God's penalty for the enormity of man's sin seemed to require nothing less than a death penalty. Early man, in and out of Jewry, wasn't unaware of this and sought to offer an offended Deity a substitute in his place. That substitute was expected to be something that man exceedingly treasured!

The greatest King of Judaism could say: 'I will not offer to the Lord my God offerings which cost me nothing.' Abraham on Mount Moriah was fully prepared to offer his only legitimate son and heir, the very idol of his life! God intervened and provided a ram as a substitute at 'the eleventh hour' (Genesis 22:13). Christians recognise this as prefiguring the lamb of God, the Creator's nearest and dearest, who was to be offered in the fullness of time upon Mount Calvary and Mount Moriah are thought by some to be the same spot.

The same message of atonement lies behind God's rejection of Cain's offering of human achievement with that of Abel's of a life from God. While the earlier incident concerning the inability of our first parents to cover their guilt and shame before a holy God conveys a similar meaning.

The biblical message was that because of disobedience to God, death entered (Ezekiel 18:4 & Romans 6:23). And whereas Divine Justice has been sore offended and demands a just penalty, Divine Love volunteers to cover what mankind is impotent to accomplish (compare Genesis 3:7 with 3:21).

Secondly, another strand throughout Old Testament history makes its presence increasingly felt. It is an evolving morality which became linked with the early seers of school of prophets. This evolving moral concern began to clash with the primitive priestly practices. The prophets rather than the priests were to become a moral mouthpiece for God; indeed, they became the champions of the oppressed. Let two such passages suffice:

'Hear the word of the Lord, you rulers of Sodom! Give ear to the teaching of our God, you people of Gomorah! What to me is the multitude of your sacrifices? says the Lord. I have more than enough of burnt offerings, of rams and the fat of animals. I have no pleasure in the blood of bulls and lambs and goats. When you come to meet with me who asked this of you?' (Isaiah 1:10-12)

'With what shall I come before the Lord and bow down before the exalted God. Shall I come before Him with burnt offerings, with calves a year old? Will the Lord be pleased with thousands of rams, with ten thousand rivers of oil? Shall I offer my firstborn for my transgression, the fruit of my body for the sin of my soul? He has showed you O man, what is good. And what does the Lord require of you? To act justly and to love mercy and to walk humbly with your God.' (Micah 6:6-8)

Through the complimentary light of the New Testament, we know that the only offering of any life to atone for our sins and indeed, the sins of the whole world, is God's offering of His very own Son (Hebrews 10:4-14)! And the message of those greater prophets of that old dispensation was that morality and mercy were of importance to God rather than rite and ritual.

Jesus, although He ultimately fulfilled the role of both sacrificial priest and victim (by the offering of Himself) came in the line of the prophets. (Luke 24:19). He was the champion of the oppressed; He came to preach deliverance to the captives (Luke 4:18). As regards current sacrificial systems of worship, He denounced them more than once (Matthew 9:13) and Matthew 12:7)! As for the moral law, He summed it up in two sayings: 'Love the Lord your God..... And your neighbour as yourself!' Neighbourliness, of course, was far more embracing to Him than it was to them: it paved the way to break the limits and barriers of racism, but only to the extent that His contemporaries could comprehend it. To break through the barriers of speciesism is but an extension of the process He began! In a sense, it is not so much what Jesus did then that counts; but in the light of what we assume He then said and did, deducing from it what He would do in today's society, if He were present with us here and now in the flesh!

Jesus, with the peasant classes in first century Palestine, would have shared His home with the beasts of burden. Usually, the only partition was a slightly raised floor between the two quarters. Bearing this in mind, plus the truth that the first creatures to share Our Lord's nativity with Joseph and Mary were traditionally an ox and an ass (Isaiah 1:3), it is easy to understand why Jesus' affinity with animals should have continued throughout His earthly sojourn. He had acquired an all-perceptive eye to perceive nature – animal as well as human!

Jesus had no need to attend a rabbinical establishment to further – nay, hinder His spiritual knowledge! To Him, the whole of life was vibrant with meaning, and the same Heavenly Father who cared for the sparrow of the tree, and the flower of the field, cared for Gentile as well as Jew. As for knowledge of human nature, no one knew what made man tick, more than did Jesus. 'He had spent the first part of His life, not shut away in places of earthly wisdom to be conditioned, but weighing up nature first hand in the carpenter's shop in Nazareth, and when He was there He would notice many an animal suffering under an unequal wooden yoke. I'm sure He still had them in mind, as well as humans, when He said: 'For my yoke is easy and my burden is light' (Matthew 11:28-30)! Yes, I've no doubt that He would have a wonderful way with those creatures of burden there that, somehow, they never forgot Him.

Years later, when His frightful passion began on that first Palm Sunday, He had become so acquainted with the animal Kingdom – and they had so come to trust Him – that He was able to mount an animal that had never been ridden before! Do you remember reading about it? (see Mark 11:1-10).

Imagine anyone else mounting an ass that hadn't been 'broken in'! See Him, guiding it up the dusty track while crowds who had gathered threw their cloaks before it while others threw down branches of palm! And think of all the waving, shouting, and possible mass hysteria yet the dear animal never bolted or panicked! You see, God was in control of the situation; He was guiding it upwards to the Holy Jerusalem.

We perceive in Jesus an acute observer of animal life, and one who had deeply learned to love the same. His perceptions were not to be blinded and distorted as were those of a later Paul of Tarsus.

The latter, though a giant of the pilgrim Church, was tainted by the distortions of worldly academies. Such an apostle would willingly distort and misquote an Old Testament reference within the very law of God itself: a biblical ruling made it clear that a beast that tramples out the corn was worthy of feeding from it, but poor Paul could hardly appreciate its relevance, and preferred to use it as applicable to humans alone (Corinthians 9:910)! Paul would hardly, then, have appreciated that the Jewish Sabbath, in one account, was for the benefit of animals as well as humans (Deuteronomy 5:14)! And it would have appeared a little absurd that legislation be given for the protection of a bird in a nest (Deuteronomy 22:6-7).

All these humane biblical laws were of little relevance to one whose sole ambition was to proclaim a dogmatic formula to humanity, the acceptance or rejection of which resulted in eternal salvation or damnation. Indeed, the urgency of Paul's uncompromising gospel was well able to periodically blind him to the injustices which permeated the larger creation in which he faithfully laboured.

Yes, as has been touched upon, the world of Jesus was far less sophisticated than Paul's. To Jesus, the wonderful 'peasant of peasants' from the poor and illiterate parts of Palestine, the whole of life was vibrant with meaning. Jesus knew that the same Heavenly Father who fed the ravens and mourned at the loss of the sparrow, even the fifth one that was 'thrown in' without any value (compare Matthew 10:29 with Luke 12:6!), could be trusted to care for fretting, anxious humans: (Luke 12:6-7).

Said the robin to the sparrow: I would
really like to know,
why those anxious human beings rush
around and worry so".
Said the sparrow to the robin: "Friend I
think that it must be,
that they have no heavenly Father such as
cares for you and me". (Anon)

Of course, why the life of one believer should be of more value than many sparrows is something we cannot answer. Let those who would quibble over such a question also ask themselves why they use many vegetables to keep alive one beast! – for is it not probable that vegetables and forms of plant life respond to feelings too?

A much more difficult passage concerns Christ's willingness to 'exorcise' one human at the cost of no less than 2000 swine being 'possessed'! The reference is to the Healing of Legion (Mark 5:9) and one confesses it to be – on the surface – the most difficult of Scripture passages as it turns docile swine into a vast herd of demon-possessed cattle who take their lives. Obviously, such a story was given to convey a moral – that the residents placed more value on their livelihood than on a restored human, and consequently they called on Christ to leave their district! The event is not recorded verbatim and there is considerable variation as given by the synoptists (see also Matthew 8:28 and Luke 8:30). Here it seems most obvious that later interpretation, as well as contemporary views of mental illness, form a strong part of it.

From a Freudian viewpoint one might say that the utterance of "Legion" and "... we are many" is the reliving of a past trauma concerning buried repression from childhood expressive of the horrible, brutal, sadistic Roman Legions. Through empathy and transference with Jesus, the man is in the throes of a severe abreaction, and as he gives vocal expression to it all the swine nearby stampede. Regrettably it is far too easy for them at such a spot to stumble over a cliff or precipice, and the result of such bolting is that a vast number landed in the sea. Current belief had it that not only was mental illness frequently caused by demonic possession, but a sure way to destroy a demon was to drown it in deep water (see e.g. Matthew 18:6)!

The above interpretation the writer owes to the late Leslie Weatherhead who used complimentary arts of hypnotherapy and analysis, as **he** does with his vocation as a minister of the gospel. He finds the interpretation most feasible, for fuller explanation see 'It happened in Palestine' – by L Weatherhead or 'Psychology, Religion and Healing' – by the same author.

Jesus, the friend of children, of outcast folk and no doubt of animals too, is (as was previously mentioned) fittingly referred to as the lamb of God, for He was tender, gentle and at the last, sacrificed. He was also 'the lion of the tribe of Judah', and whereas His lamb-like meekness was manifested to the lowly, He could equally manifest the strength and destructiveness of a lion towards the hypocrites and exploiters of His time. Indeed, if the 'Triumphal Entry', touched upon earlier, was a mark of His meekness, then the Cleansing of the Temple which followed on from it was a mark of His ferocity! But then I refer to the Johanine account of an almost identical occurrence, an earlier cleansing of the same Temple. Near the beginning of Jesus' ministry, we find Him making a whip and not only showing physical violence but uprooting or overturning the tables of the money changers (as narrated by the Synoptists). But we also read of how on this earlier occasion He used the scourge to liberate the animals from the precincts.

Consequently, they were freed from being from being sold for ritual sacrifice (John 2:15).

It is obvious, therefore, whether we like it or not, that Jesus of Nazareth was not only a law breaker, guilty of civil disobedience, but on this occasion an animal liberator. Let us then as professed followers of the Nazarene, see to it that we do not unduly criticise those of the animal liberation front who get 'carried away' by a righteous indignation! If we got more infuriated against the brutality they oppose, it might say more for us! Oh how easy it is for all of us to criticise the zeal in others that we ourselves lack and to find rationalisation for our own cowardice! There are times of exception when loyalty to the highest laws will necessitate us breaking lesser laws.

In Jesus, the Christ, we have the most militant of people as well as the most meek, and He was The Master of every situation. We, as sinful mortals, are also made up of differing drives. Freud once referred to the oral, anal, pregenital and phallic stages. Jung spoke in terms of the conscious and the shadow, as well as of the extrovert and introvert drives. One thing was sure about Jesus: He knew when to give expression to the Lamb as well as to the lion! We who follow as disciples must learn to do likewise. Those who cannot control or direct their emotions, as those who become victims of mass hysteria, can be of little service in the work of the Animal Rights movements. We need to be conscious of our own weaknesses and susceptibilities, as well as shrewd observers of others. Like Jesus, we must become 'as wise as serpents and as harmless as doves' (Matthew 10:16).

Yes, He undoubtedly knew the characteristics of animals as well as humans: He knew that Pharisees were as venomous as the snakes (Matthew 23:33) and He was able to refer to Herod, tongue in cheek, as "that old fox" (Luke 13:32)!

Yes, animals should have rights, but let no supporter confine evil, stealth and guile to humanity. We live in a 'fallen' world. The whole of creation is not as soft and loving as pussy is towards her mistress, but rather what she chooses to be towards mice or birds before her path! Jesus was at every stage a realist; so later was Paul when He cast a venomous snake, which has presumably bitten him, into a fire (Acts 28:5). The Bible largely distinguishes between 'beasts' and 'brute beasts'. A contrast, indeed, to Dostoevsky who wrote: 'do not exalt yourself above the animals: **they are**

without sin'! One wonders how many of the fiercer variety he'd actually encountered. As for the gentler, they can frequently appear as guilt ridden, when trying to 'cover up', as any child!

We have touched briefly, yet with relevance, on what Jesus was like when He was with us in the flesh. That is what He expects the Church to be like now that He is in Heaven! He was a stirrer of the people, and His first century followers were, consequently, accused of turning the world upside-down (Acts 17:6). As He was militant so was the early Church that followed. But today, the body of Christ on earth is as far removed from His militance as the South Pole is from the North. Yet, traditional Anglicans – loyal to their Book of Common Prayer – pray week after week 'for the Church **militant** here on earth'!

As mentioned previously, in earlier Biblical times a divergence between the priestly and prophetic ministries had become apparent. Prophets, with their moral impetus, and priests also, with their molten idols, had existed and practised their differing roles within the very same communities. Jesus was not alone in taking upon Himself the heritage of the prophet, for so did His followers. As the prophets had been stoned because of the utterance of their lips, so would the Son of God suffer crucifixion.

Jesus, nearing the end of His Ministry, prepared His disciples through prophetic symbolism, for His own departure from them. He took bread and wine, and it is 'possible' that He partook of the Passover Lamb, though it is questionable due to His criticism of sacrificial ritual already touched on. Yet we have no more right to twist Our Lord into a vegetarian mould than others might, one of a total abstainer! Indeed, the lengths to which some Christian sects will go to get Jesus pigeon-holed into their own preconceived moral moulds is quite remarkable!

One thing we do know is that during the next day Jesus was crucified because of the way He had used his tongue, but miracle of miracles, death could literally never hold such a good person down. He arose from the dead, and a few days later, just to prove that He was more than a mere apparition, Jesus not only broke bread, but at the seaside He prepared some fish for those disciples who were to become fishers of men! One matter of true consolation is that the fish of that period were caught in nets! The abominable practice today of ripping a poor creature's mouth by a hook is far removed from fishing nets in Bible fashion. Of course, whether creatures that wriggle on the shore, deprived of water, are really suffering, none of us can know. We presume they **are** – as we do the little fish they eat alive! The writer well remembers that while on holiday off the Welsh Gower coast, he and his children spent futile hours in a far distant summer, casting little fish back into the water but never fast enough for them to return to the shore. It seemed as if they were anxious to surrender life! Whether we approve or not, we are also perpetually consuming marine life in the water we drink and, alas, boiling it as well!

On what might appear a brighter note, it is worth of consideration that though Jesus may indeed have gone up to attend feasts at Jerusalem, it appears that what The Saviour taught others He expressed by His own example: "The time cometh and now is when the true worshippers shall worship in spirit and in truth" (John 4:21-24).

Yes, the older priestly line has its fulfilment in the costliest and most heart rendering sacrifice of all when Jesus – the long-awaited Lamb of God - offers His life in expiation for ours – this is the Good News of the Old Time Gospel, and in 'The Nazarene' we have the zenith of prophetic zeal – He lashes the exploiters and the oppressors with His tongue, and fulfils a ministry of liberating the captives. There remains last but not least His pastoral (shepherd's) role – partly the outcome of a first-class knowledge of Scripture, and equally the influence of home life and background.

Right Priorities

We have discussed most of the relevant Scriptures, but we have far from exhausted them. There are indeed more, and some are worthy of special consideration in that they express more forcefully still the Christian need of right priorities. In the moral sphere it is so easy to get wrapped up with the trivial and to overlook the truly important issues of life. Perhaps the worst crime of the Pharisees which made them guilty of utter hypocrisy was that morally, they squeezed out gnats while they swallowed camels (Matthew 23:24). You will find, as has already been briefly touched upon, that Christendom today is guilty of the very same hypocrisy. Much steam is generated as well as space and time given to such issues as forms of ministry and liturgy, while all around the helpless are being brutally exploited – and that they should happen to be of a different species does not absolve us from blame. God's compassion and benevolence embraces the whole of His creation and we are called to be faithful stewards (1 Corinthians 4:2).

To learn of right priorities in God's sight we need do no more than find out the top or most frequently used analogy the Scriptures give us of Our Maker. We might equally consider how Christ most forcefully expressed it in himself. Indeed, you have no doubt reached the solution already! As for the prime analogy concerning the Creator and His care of the creation, it is in terms of an eastern shepherd's care for His sheep. It is the pastoral role mentioned. The most popular of all the psalms – the twenty third – expresses it beautifully. It was written hundreds of years previous to Jesus, by that Shepherd King and sweet psalmist of old, David. This 'analogy supreme' is that God's love and care of His people is comparable to an Israelite shepherd's love and care of his sheep. Many such references are to be found in both Testaments of Scripture, though none is as well-known as this twenty third psalm. It is actually sung in metre to the Scottish tune Crimond more than any hymn in the world!

The resulting popularity of the 23rd psalm however, must never blind us to other equally beautiful passages of Scripture, such as:

'He will feed his flock like a shepherd,
He will carry the lambs in His arms,
He will carry them in His bosom, and
Gently lead those that are with young'

Isaiah chapter 40:11-12

When we come to the New Testament, Jesus Himself takes up the same theme. This is so wonderfully expressed in the Gospel according to John where our Master identified Himself with the role of a good shepherd. Throughout this Gospel Jesus frequently draws on the analogy, and at the end He commissions Peter to fulfil such a calling, with regard to young as well as old (John 21:15-17).

Indeed, the very Church today still takes up the pastoral theme – hence a bishop's crook! But so debased has husbandry become today that this most prominent of Divine analogies – indeed, as mentioned in a Bible concordance no less than eighty times – is fast becoming inadequate and irrelevant. For example, to equate oneself with a sheep and say, 'The Lord is my intensive sheep breeder, I shall not want', would be blasphemous and totally untrue.

The fact that the analogy of a shepherd's care was the most frequent one used of God in the Bible is the greatest compliment those far off shepherds could ever have been paid. Is it then to be wondered at that when Jesus was born in Bethlehem, the class of persons singled out to witness His birth were shepherds? Wise men later witnessed a star. But shepherds received a delegation of angels sent from God while they were caring for animals at night! It is the writer's contention that to those who watch over helpless creatures, in the dark night of this present world, angels of God still manifest themselves!

The writer knows this: that the most saintly people he has come across has been since he has joined the ranks of animal activists, and though many of them may not acknowledge Christ by name, they do so in deed. The French philosopher Maritain once wrote: 'Wherever there is genuine goodness, there is Christ whether we know him by name or not! And there is much truth in that simple statement. Those who openly profess Christianity for an ulterior motive, even though the motive be no less than the salvation of their souls, have hardly evolved to the same plane as those who care for the defenceless of this world without any desire of reward. The moral contrast between the pompous, perverted prelate, limiting God's compassion and concern to his own Denomination and claiming spiritual superiority, with that of many a lowly animal liberationist working away secretly in the dark so as to break into an animal Belsen so as to 'liberate the captives', conveys its own message. Rescuing animals from the vivisectors trap is, figuratively speaking, the mark of a true shepherd's care!

Though good shepherds were despised by the rabbinical classes of first century Palestine as ignorant, they were chosen and precious in God's eyes. Jesus knowing of their willingness to go in search for a lost animal, and if necessary, lay down their lives for the same, resulted in Him proudly identifying Himself with them (John 10:1-18).

Admittedly, not every shepherd was good to his flock but exceptions were considered rare. The instance of such a rarity is used in scripture as an analogy of faithless Pastors – indeed Ezekiel's prophecy gives such an example – (Ezekiel 34:1-16). This passage is a reminder of God's wrath and indignation towards wicked husbandmen, and the passage is vibrant with a Divine compassion towards the creatures that have been abused and exploited.

In the light of the above, just where, as a Church, are our moral priorities today? Are we as near the heart of God as were those good shepherds of both Old and New Testaments? Is our care for cattle as compassionate, loving and caring as were those husbandmen of two to three millenniums previous? God save us! We stand condemned as guilty, as unashamed exploiters of the dumb creation. Indeed, so far have we stooped and degraded ourselves here, that instances are known when animals are deliberately made dumb by vivisectors, and this with the approval of self-styled Christian government's approval. The groaning of such victims can only be heard by God Himself and the perpetrators assume they can be pardoned. As far as priestly absolution is concerned, there is no problem, nevertheless, "Vengeance is mine, I will repay, saith the Lord" (Hebrews 10:30). Justice demands a hell as well as a heaven!

Much sadism abominably receives the veneer of religious approval and the words of Jeremiah still seem relevant: "And my people love to have it so!" (Jeremiah 5:31). The mortal sin of a Catholic missing Mass on a Sunday or a holy day of obligation, still receives the condemnation of that Church. To drink alcohol, doubt the virgin birth, utter four letter words, or blaspheme, might equally result in ostracism from many a Reformed or Protestant Church. But the torture of animals for human vanity, scientific experimentation or food is considered quite acceptable and hardly void of moral and spiritual offence. Instances abound: The writer attended a religious retreat next to a farm; it proved most difficult listening to the Nun's meditation on 'sanctity' because of the constant mooing of cows from a farm almost adjacent. The mothers had just had their calves removed from them and such inarticulate groaning conveyed its own story! The writer just couldn't partake of milk in the beverage that followed this 'Holy Hour', but others had no problem. They were more intrigued that brown cows ate green grass to produce white milk! As the creatures provided far more than was necessary for the time spent with their young, the implication was that humans were doing them a favour in helping them to get rid of their surplus. How the cream of professions had been conned! As for the less analytical types, well 'where ignorance is bliss it is folly to be wise!' There is a price to be paid for true enlightenment which most of us are unprepared to pay.

Jesus was fully aware of how the theology of His day and those responsible for it, was a moral distortion. The very word 'sinner' had a different meaning to Him than it had to them – for example, in Matthew chapter 9:13 the context reveals Jesus in the company of 'sinners'! For these 'holier than thous' a sinner, among other things, could be one who was ignorant of the law; a blatant breaker of it; or possibly a member of another race through no fault of his own! That a man claiming the role of a prophet should share a meal with such 'irreligious' folk was to rank Him as being as ungodly as they were. The weightier matters of caring for the underprivileged, helping the fallen and protecting the defenceless were virtues little perceived by those first century 'moral perverts of respectability'. Such were the religious leaders during Christ's earthly ministry, and Christendom is top heavy with them today!

Similarly, if we turn to Matthew 12:1-7 we find it considered wicked to pluck ears of corn on a Sabbath while strolling through the fields. The implication was that this involved working on the Day of Rest! This again was an instance of the 'moral authorities' making mountains out of molehills while they, undoubtedly, shrank mountains into molehills! No wonder Jesus and the religious elite couldn't continue side by side; they were as diametrically opposed to Him as darkness is to light, and Christendom today isn't one iota different from them. Moral standards amongst the religious are still extremely topsy-turvy.

It can equally be said with justification that the very term 'sin', or the practiser of it – sinner, is as morally distorted a term today as it was in the first century. To blaspheme, disbelieve doctrine, have extra-marital relationships, curse the Pope or even use a Durex, would undoubtedly be to act sinfully. To be regular at worship, free from blasphemy, and say the Rosary or read the Bible each night, would be the marks of religious piety and goodness! To be decent, well that's largely a matter of making everyone at home in your company, never rocking the boat or uttering an uncomfortable statement; it also concerns attire, like keeping your tie straight. To have a fly button unfastened, or do without a bra, is to act indecently! The pressure is on you to conform to contemporary fads (and it's surprising how they can change!). Jesus, however, wouldn't. He was the greatest nonconformist of all. That is why they considered Him indecently irreligious. THAT is why the crucified Him!

Religious morality isn't one iota better today than it was two millenniums ago. Its meaning has very largely been shrunk to the expression of sexual factors. A woman who buys and wears a mink coat while fully conversant with the cruelty involved in its manufacture is hardly likely for that reason to be classed as immoral. Should she wear it regularly at Church from which she scarcely misses a service, she will generally be classed a religiously upright and moral. A dear woman who, on the contrary, would oppose all forms of animal brutality, (and for that reason never wear a fur coat), yet happens to indulge in open sexual activity with all and sundry, would not only be castigated as a slut but as appallingly immoral. Yes, sin and sex degenerated into almost changeable terms; the result of sub apostolic eras to be touched on in the next chapter.

This writer knew of a Welsh famer whose morality was so high that should he have come across a farmhand uttering blasphemies, then the man could well have been dismissed. Four letter words or smutty jokes would likewise have been severely censored. The farmer was an ardent lay-preacher around the Chapels of the vicinity. However, to visit his livestock was to be confronted by battery cages and veal pens, where birds and animals were deprived the basic right of bodily movement. Yet conditions such as these would hardly have appeared to the man as immoral. The dear man was not fully to blame: he was the outcome of a conditioned religious morality of which the Churches have an overload. One could affirm that such contemporary morality was on a par with that of a bygone age when 'God fearing employers chained up their slaves in the outbuildings at the end of a busy day and then retired to the family hearth to lead family prayers and read the 'Good Book'!

It is not uncommon to find more affluent 'religious houses' occasionally carving up veal for a festive dinner, to be consumed by the residents and guests during religious silence – broken only by a devotional reading being given on piety and virtue!

But then, sometimes we need go no further than our own home! Many religious families discuss the themes of worship, sanctity and holiness while they cut into their factory produced farm food or crack open their battery eggs! But then 'religion' to many people is little more than the association of musty smells and atmospheres one associates with buildings used for worship. The 'saintly' are equated with those attached to them who wear long robes, speak in a quiet tone, and recite liturgies repetitively. One's dealing and treatment of helpless creatures from a differing species is something considered inappropriate to such an ethos. A dog wandering into a religious building would be speedily removed by 'horror stricken' worshippers. In the Bible, the term dogs could, undoubtedly, have allusions to fierce scavengers which prowled around at night; and was used in a non literal sense of male prostitutes – e.g. Revelation 22:15. However, there were also the domesticated kind; many of which were household pets (Mark 7:28 & possibly Luke 16:21).

Those of a High Church orientation are not the only culprits guilty of ejecting animals from Christendom's ark. Low Church evangelicalism, which is increasing the most, is equally as guilty. Indeed, when the writer expressed his abhorrence of animal exploitation in the presence of an evangelical brother, the reply was "Don't get side-tracked from the only message that counts, brother. Our sole task is to save souls for Jesus!" Well, if 'getting folk saved' made them more compassionate and concerned about the rest of creation I'd shout 'Hallelujah!!' every time. As it is, my sympathies lie with the comment made by Anna Sewell, authoress of BLACK BEAUTY:

'There is no religion without love, and
People may talk as much as they like about
their religion, but if it does not teach
them to be good and kind to animals as well
as humans, it is all a sham'

The author, while attending an Evangelical Conference many years ago, touched upon animal cruelty and the Church's need to reclaim the spirit of St Francis. His utterance was followed by a chuckle which reverberated. One cleric rose up to express the feeling of the rest: "What on earth has the Holy Spirit to do with **animals!**" Yes, it was obvious. They were only concerned with 'speaking in tongues'; swaying in unison with the jiggy tunes which caused a 'trickle down the spine'; and healing manifestations claimed to be divine, but in reality, induced by hypnotic effect. One dear soul could only assume in the writer's despondency a lack of spiritual life. She expressed it either in blunt Yorkshire or Lancashire: "You need your baptism in the Spirit Bro, 'it's better felt than telt'"

Such glossolalia as is frequent in these so-called, 'spirit filled' assemblies is usually no more ethical than has been expressed by dancing dervishes. The first king of Israel was gullible to them (1 Samuel 10:11). Thankfully, with the evolvement of an ever-growing moral concept of God, the later characters of such a line express Divine inspiration no longer by behaviour characteristic of hysteria, but by becoming a moral mouthpiece for the defenceless of their era. They manifested a fearlessness and a boldness on behalf of the exploited which could frequently bring tyrants and despots to their knees. Such a worthy line began in prominence with Nathan and his story about a pet lamb. It culminated with John the Baptist (11 Samuel 12:1-3 and Matthew 11:9-11).

Those of the truly prophetic line, and their successors – the Wilberforces, the Lincolns and the Gandhis – are the truly 'Spirit Filled'. Unfortunately, too many times the church has been a fruit and nut case: too little fruit and too many nuts! The Master made it clear: "By their fruits ye shall know them." (Matthew 7:15-23).

The fisher folk, amongst whom the writer lives, are basically very caring and deeply religious. The morals of a small section of them are, however, exceedingly narrow. The present writer, in a biography of his, soon to be published, mentions a one-night stand with a lady of the streets when he was hardly twenty-one. The tabloid press delighted in publicising this, out of context. Consequently, a small but vociferous moral outburst of indignation followed. Its impetus came from an area where **live** crabs and lobsters are constantly being 'slowly brought to the boil' for human consumption. Presumably there is nothing wrong in that! I wonder if these prim and proper folk are singing 'What a friend we have in Jesus' as they go about their macabre task, pushing down the creatures further into the water as the pot approaches the boil!

The God of biblical revelation is a Deity whose domain and rule can never be confined to humanity. He upholds the whole of life. It is never unaware of His presence. Yes, the fish included (Job 12:1-10)!

And whatever one might think of fishing, catching shellfish to boil them alive could **never** have been the prior occupation of those who became fishers of men (Leviticus 11:9-12)!

In claiming an exclusive relationship with God, man does the Creator a great injustice. And as if this is not enough, he distorts His ethical priorities. Man – supposedly speaking for God – magnifies moral midges while he minimises moral camels. Yes, like their first century predecessors, religious leaders today are guilty of portraying the Deity as quite puny and perverted in His values. A contrast, indeed, to what we've already learnt from biblical passages already quoted, with far more to follow.

Retrograde Processes

The Hebrews had taught that there was a very real place within a restored Paradise, if not a future Millennium, for animals. Indeed, their Scriptures had also taught that animals came under the caring eye of God in this present interim life. The New Testament continues with such an outlook, taught and expressed by the Good Shepherd, and though it is briefly touched upon by Paul, it is fully expressed in the eschatology of the last book, attributed to John. All these factors have been touched on. Indeed, one would have expected such a growing spiritual concept to have further evolved, after the close of our Biblical canon, but this was not to be. Indeed, around this early era we discern the commencement of what was to become two diverging paths in the history of Christendom – the one eventually looking back for moral criteria, the other moving forward, while a large branch of the latter weds itself to Pagan philosophy.

The former strand became a biblical Christianity for, after the completion of a Biblical canon around the fourth century, it barred itself from evolving to any higher level of morality than that which had been delivered once and for all (supposedly at the end of time) to the saints! (Jude

3). These saints had now gone to their reward but not without leaving their approved list of writings. "What do the Scriptures say?" became the criteria. Indeed, such a sacred volume was so complete in itself that only God Himself could seemingly have brought about such a dove-tailed, compact and perfected volume! And as if to confirm its finality, a curse was contained in the last chapter of the final book towards any who would dare to add to it: "Whoever adds to the things contained, to him shall be added the plagues herein!" (Rev. 22:18).

These groups of Christians who followed a Bible-orientated life were to become persecuted minorities for refusing to respect the pagan trends and coercive power of a larger branch of Christendom. Indeed, much of what we have learnt about these early Bible Christians is slanted. It has come down from their ecclesiastical opponents who used the carnal weapons of this world to subjugate their rivals into submission.

Many of these gatherings of the Faithful were severely supressed only to revive at a later date under a variety of labels appended by their antagonists. There were the Albigenses, Waldenses, Anabaptists and Moravians. And, later still the Lutherans, Anglicans, Presbyterians, Congregationalists and Baptists. We have reactionary movements such as Unitarians, Quakers and then Methodists. And more recent still, the Brethren groups, the Four Square Pentecostal groups, and at present the charismatic renewal and house church efforts. Yet the cry is basically the same, whether it be given by Billy Graham, a Peter Waldo or a John Huss: "The Bible says!" and the emphasis is always 'Back' to the Bible!

Fortunately for the dumb creation, as we have well seen, the Bible has a very great deal to convey about the Creator's attitude towards animals. As a consequence, Bible orientated believers will show quite an element of compassion to the brute beasts of the fields, but of course no more than that taught in the inspired volume. The basic weakness of such theology is that it usually regards the religious volume as 'equally' inspired from cover to cover. It fails to perceive it for what it basically is: a collection of literature scanning the vast period of an ancient Nation's religious history, which was frequently modified, re-edited and reformulated through a uniquely inspired experiential knowledge of God. Regrettably for many this Bible, rather than becoming a seed bed from which ethical values will continue to grow, becomes a brake upon any moral advancement beyond itself!

In the light of the above, it is to be wondered at that the burning of witches, the stoning of adulteresses, and a host of other barbaric practices have been perpetuated by God-fearing folk! Because of such a theology Reformers like Wilberforce were sometimes denounced by Christians for abolishing slavery – a practice condoned in parts of scripture! In more recent times one or two isolated scriptural passages have similarly been cited to bolster up the system of apartheid. Perhaps, quite remarkably, the exception to the rule has been the general monogamy of the Christian world – for polygamy was largely the norm with affluent Bible personalities! Although the penalty for adultery was death, many people acquired with religious approval, several wives – plus a multitude of concubines to go with them! Such Scripturally backed moral permissiveness, however, is hardly used by Bible Christians today. Most see in the Book what they want to see, and no more!

The second strand of Christendom, that which refused to be bound by the strictures of a religious volume, was to eventually disrupt between east and west: Orthodox and Latin. The latter, at a later period, assumed (quite wrongly) that she had brought about the Canon of Scripture and, consequently, was never ever bound by it. Her emphasis was that the Holy Spirit was still leading the Church into further truth. The outcome has been that truth, with the passing of time, appears contradictory! For example, the Fathers frequently contradict the Scriptures, the councils frequently contradict each other. Popes refer to people in one era as heretics fit for burning and in the same present change of climate: separated brethren of the same Church!

Fortunately for animals, an ex-cathedra statement affirming that animals have no souls could yet be superseded by a future pronouncement that they have! Nevertheless, a Church claiming infallibility is hardly likely to confess to having erred, so casuistry becomes a means of trying to get out of embarrassingly tight corners! Thankfully, the spiritually astute see all this for what it is. Nothing less than a sheer mass of blundering hypocrisy.

This section of the early Church which refused to be bound by the limits of a completed canon of Scripture – a Bible, certainly evolved spiritually in several quarters. After a split occasioned through further claims from the

Roman bishop (and later backed by forged decretals), the eastern branch – terming itself Orthodox – created many saints whose love and care of the animal creation is a credit to it.

There were saints such as Basil the Great who compiled a beautiful prayer which includes animals as well as humans. We have the wonderful writings which come down from Isaic the Syrian. There is the better-known John Chrysostom, and indeed there are many more. Whether such stories however are fact or fiction is highly questionable. But, if nothing else, they portray an acknowledgement of close affinity between man and beast sadly lacking throughout later Christendom.

As for the western branch of this early church – calling itself catholic – it so absorbed the spirit of Imperial Rome as to imitate its ruthlessness. The once persecuted now became the persecutor. And the theology it would formulate later would not be the heritage of a Hebrew Christian other worldliness. In winning the world it was becoming captive to its prevailing philosophic concepts. Indeed, Roman Catholicism would evolve as a syncretism of Christianity from Palestine with the cosmology and philosophy of an Aristotle from Greece! And all this, for the animal creation, would result in utter disaster. Yes, all the more tragic when one considers earlier saints of this Latin church who had been so caring towards them.

The greatest gift this earlier Catholicism has given Western Christendom is Francis of Assisi. Stories of his dealings with non-humans would fill many pages. But alas, the very year that the godly Francis died a very different character was born. This was Thomas Aquinas, who later received the nickname of 'The Angelic Doctor'. Indeed, the title was most inappropriate; one need only consider his 'Summa Theologica's' interpretation of animal life. Nothing acted more as a brake on the new influence of the godly Francis than the eventual publication of Thomas Aquinas's unfinished work. This was supposed to contain the whole of the Christian religion, from the existence of God to the very precepts of morality – with all conceivable objection stated and answered. It occupied the last nine years of Aquinas's earthly life and was, very largely, the adoption of Aristotelian philosophy into a religious system, so as to become the latter's apologetics.

The sacred Scriptures had already warned about the vain philosophies of this world – of the danger of being deluded by them. (Cor. 2:8). Now the Roman Church had become so much one with the world that under the influence of the 'Angelic Doctor' it not only exalted the pagan Aristotle as **the** Philosopher, but it also imbibed into its system the jurisprudence of Pagan Rome!

The above factors were to 'snuff out' of the authoritarian Western Church any compassion or consideration towards the animal creation. Greek philosophy idolised the mental while it debased the physical. It was assumed that animals were purely sensual creatures – brute beasts of carnality denied of a so-called immortal soul which humans alone possessed. As 'rights' were only given to Roman persons (persona), animals, as mere things, were only created for men to use. One had no moral obligation towards a thing; you can only sin towards a person! Consequently, as C.W.Hume so aptly put it: "the broad minded, realistic, generous neighbourliness which the Bible exhibited came to be replaced by a narrow spirit of academic anthropocentricity". Yes, the Roman Church had chosen a Thomist in preference to a Francis. As a consequence, not only would the animals suffer greatly, so would the Galileos who questioned an Aristotelian cosmology.

Hans Ruesch, similarly, expresses the degradation of Roman Catholic morality at the above stage: "St Thomas Aquinas whose anthropocentric teachings flattered human vanity and justified the vast abuse of animals, provided a doctrinal basis for the church's contempt of animals, and for deriding St Francis of Assisi's invocations that animals are worthy of man's respect and love."

Yes, thanks to the corrupt and contaminating influence of Scholasticism, Schopenhauer could later write, "Christian morality contains the great and essential imperfection of taking into consideration only man, and leaving the entire animal world without rights."

Yes, and such contagion has been carried over into much of the Protestant world where no place whatever is given for animals in its liturgies or intercessions. A marked departure indeed, from the psalmtry of the Old Testament era, the very closing verse of which is, "Let everything that breathes Praise the Lord. Allelujah!" (Psalm 50:2)

The Roman branch of Christendom took yet another retrograde step, for though it later put Galileo to silence (the threat of torture by the Inquisition led even the bravest to recant!), it seemingly brought no such threats against a contemporary, Rene Descartes! This man was not only to be termed 'The Father of Modern Philosophy', but as Francis Schaeffer reminds us 'A Good Catholic'. The same individual publicly perpetrated in his teaching that because animals lack intellect and language there is no way of distinguishing them from machines.

Hume reminds us that with the followers of Descartes the attitude and philosophy towards animals touched rock bottom in the seventeenth century. His followers, the Cartesians, 'dissected dogs without pity to observe the circulation of the blood. One of them (Malebranche), as he gave his dog a fierce kick in the presence of others, added: "What? Don't you know that it doesn't feel?" What in fact were the screams? 'Simply the creaking of the gearing and the runspit!'

Barbarity such as the above was 'the outcome of a philosophy which identified the human soul or consciousness so completely with reason as to conclude that animals could not be conscious at all, and were in fact just automata' (Animals and Why They Matter, by Mary Midgely).

There was no Papal denunciation for such a loyal catholic as Descartes! Indeed, it is to be an Atheist we turn for protest and repudiation of such reasoning: "You discover in it all the same organs of feeling that are in yourself. Answer me, mechanist, has nature arranged all the means of feeling in this animal so that it may **not** feel?" (Voltaire to a vivisector – from his Philosophical Dictionary).

Need one wonder that with Catholicism condoning such philosophies the Latin Nations became notorious for callousness and brutality towards animals! You could inflict cruelty upon a beast with moral impunity, but to miss Mass on a Sunday or any Holy Day of obligation could well be a mortal sin. Unabsolved by priestly absolution, their theology taught that you would spend eternity in Hell rather than centuries in purgatory!

So divorced has piety become from true Christian morality as seen in Scripture that many who today manufacture 'paté de fois gras' in France will be regular attenders at Mass. In earlier times their predecessors would frequently cease, momentarily, from bludgeoning cattle while they observed the Angelus!

The toreador in Spain will seek the priestly blessing before the bullfight, and at the end of the barbaric spectacle, his ceremonial cloak may well drape the statue of the Madonna. And though as far back as 1567 Pope St Pius V formally forbade bullfights, threatened excommunication to all who organised them, and ruled out ecclesiastical burial for those who had been killed in them, a highly contrasting policy occurred as recent as 1972! For it was in that year when Pope Paul VI broke that long standing humanitarian tradition by openly welcoming and blessing a delegation of Spanish bullfighters.

Indeed, it is equally tragic to have to affirm that, the same church's largest step backwards was Her official endorsement of vivisection in 1966 by the same Pope! Indeed, this denomination which has despised animals, denying not only to them a soul but also a free will, has given her official blessing to those who torture them for the supposed benefit of an assumed Master Species. And to add insult to injury, occasional chapels exist where the perpetrators of such atrocities can, as practising vivisectors, receive priestly sacraments.

I quote yet again from Hans Ruesch – 'Slaughter of the Innocent' – which I heartily recommend to you: "A Church that barely a century ago considered it normal to celebrate All Saint's Day in Italy by burning barrels full of live cats in the town squares has contributed notably to such an attitude."

Yes, and the attitude is doctrinally unchanged. Rome lives up to her *semper eadem*. For in Spain at Easter, live birds encaged in stone pots are still suspended on poles, there to be stoned to death as part of a local ritual encouraged by parish priests. As for Italy itself, Archbishop Battisi made headlines throughout parts of the world's press when in January 1989, addressing a startled gathering he said: "To beat up a dog or leave it to die of starvation is not a sin. For a dog is not a person and therefore has no soul. So no sin is committed!"

While the Latin countries have often stunned us by their lax moral standards, countries influenced most by the Protestant Reformation have frequently suppressed us by their moral rigidity. Indeed, while parts of the Emerald Isle have drunk themselves into a stupor, other parts have denounced with no uncertainty the demon drink. And both have done it representing Christianity! I must admit, however, that I enjoy a regular pint of stout and that my conscience far less troubles me with a pint of ale, stout or pure scrumpy than it ever does with the traditional English cup of tea.

I guess I'm a contrast in real life to the clerical image I put across for the Big Breakfast Show last year! After having been called in to bless their pets I was later asked by Chris Evans: "Another cup of tea vicar?" "Ooh yes, I'd simply love another cup of tea" I replied. They told me later: 'You've really made this morning's programme, James!'. Yes, I believe I had, because the traditional cleric (about to move to new pastures) is usually missed most by convivial groups of elderly women: "We ladies will miss you most vicar. We've always felt you were one of us!", was a most appropriate reply I once overheard.

Sadly, those tea and milk drinking puritans, ever keen on denouncing alcohol are most reluctant to denounce the production of milk which whitens the nation's regular cuppa. (For that matter, they're seldom keen to denounce the working conditions of a tea plantation!) History simply repeats itself: almost 2 millennia later, religious leaders search to pick out moral midges while swallowing moral camels whole! It is undeniably a fact that over indulgence of alcohol can cause damage, but it is equally an undeniable fact that the New Testament nowhere enforces total abstinence. Yet evangelical preachers, claiming to interpret the message of Our Lord frequently do! In all fairness, one should approach the Christian scriptures willing to learn from them rather than in seeking to bolster up preconceived theories.

Because of the above, the writer admits that although using the baby food of another species to feed the adulthood of our own, is unique to the human species – and quite immoral to him – he cannot find scripture to oppose the practice. Except, of course, that reaping what we sow (Galatians 6:7) may well be reflected in the major killing diseases of our time. For are they not the outcome of the suffering we inflict daily on defenceless beasts! Indeed, vegans alone are immune (to a remarkable degree) from the same dairy produced diseases? Regardless of the counter arguments from those with vested interests in the dairy trade, veganism is but the next step up from a vegetarianism which is now established and well respected.

Living as a teenager in far off war years, the writer knew that the number one killer disease was tuberculosis. He also learned that milk was the number one conveyor of that infection! Yet, in those years the exploitation of cattle to meet the nation's dairy supply (increased by free milk in schools!) was as nothing compared to the cruelty that exists today. Much further back still - indeed as far back as biblical times – when the cow was as much a part of the home as were the humans, it was basically the surplus milk that was used for human consumption. What a contrast to the corruption and cruelty that has escalated from the vast evil of modern intensive farming supported by vested veterinary interest; and behind it all the drug industry as well as influential MPs of differing parties!

During the last decade, a local education committee were offered, and indeed accepted, the installation and use of milk vending machines within each local school. The milk marketing board were viewed as most kind and caring in offering such services free. However, when the writer as a member of that meeting suggested to the chairman (a farmer and ex MP), that provision equally be made for the alternative of pure fruit juice throughout each school, the response appeared as one of aghast surprise, silence and a moving on to the next item on the agenda.

The effects of so much dairy produce consumed – like those of a high cholesterol level – can be lethal and grave. But when one considers the intense suffering perpetrated to produce it, could justice expect otherwise? Meanwhile, the caricature of a traditional cleric daintily supping his dairy whitened 'cuppa' supposedly reflects his soberness and gentility; but in reality, it reflects the shallowness, indeed emptiness, of a character unable to read bovine eyes. Surely, if ever four-legged creatures needed a blessing from God these four-legged creatures do! But the response from a frivolous humanity, when such a blessing is given by a man of God is just as shallow: 'Holy Cow!' was a typical response I received from a light-hearted leading tabloid!

Do people not realise that the average cow is made pregnant every year; that her calf is taken from her before three days old; that she is pressed relentlessly for higher supplies of milk; indeed, that 6-7 months each year she is milked whilst pregnant; that hours of her life are on concrete floors, and soaked in her own slurry; and that the only way to ward off increasing susceptibility to disease is by a flood of antibiotic drugs purchased from the drug industry, frequently with horrid side effects? Indeed, the poor creature, once drained of milk through repetitive abuse will finally be rewarded by a journey to some distant slaughterhouse, and not infrequently via an appalling journey abroad.

When the evils of intensive factory farming were touched upon from the pulpit of the writer's first Parish, and within its Parish News (1969-70). Several regular worshippers ceased attending. One withdrew his financial support and said he would resume it when the articles and sermons were toned down. The spokesman for the group was the local vet who'd previously refused to board the Rectory pet in his kennels. "It's a mongrel!" he'd affirmed. The vet became the rector's vociferous opponent, claiming that some of his best clients had been deeply hurt.

The young Rector had been told, on arriving at this affluent parish of meanness: "If you play your cards well and don't rock the boat, you'll be settled for life!" Thankfully, he didn't succumb to such plausibility. He certainly rocked the boat, was severely hounded through sticking out his neck for the animal cause and was warned by the vet that he might well get his head knocked off in the process! Twenty four years later the writer, as a consequence, can look His Maker in the face, sense His smile and hear the song of the birds..... but later episodes in such a biography have yet to be told!

(Top) Demonstrating outside Aberdeen's Marischal College, the site of horrendous vivisection by non medics! Attached is the Greyfriars Kirk (Presbyterian), dedicated to followers of Francis Of Assisi!
(Bottom) Margaret Moir of Ellon, Nr Aberdeen, **struggles** valiantly to feed her many rescued primates. While some large groups merely beg, philosophise, compromise and reward themselves high salaries!

(Top) Mother superior at Daventry opposing mass media who, further criticize her battery establishment. Salmonella has now broken out!
 (Bottom) The quality of this reproduction is poor - a local newspaper having lost the original! - nevertheless, its message of the Daventry nuns inhumane battery establishment is pronounced.

(Top) These evil veal crates, in which baby calves stolen from their mothers were incarcerated, were used in Storrington Priory until mounting pressure from activists and the CIWF prevailed.
(Bottom) The author blessing a cow. Understandably 'Holy Cow!' was a tabloid's later report. But if any animal deserved blessing, non more than she who is so diabolically misused - for daily pintas!

(Top) Many Spanish priests support bullfights. One even teaches the 'art' as a senior instructor! The one here attired as matador, later gloated over having hacked off both ears of his victim!
(Bottom) Further results of false theology! The bull outside the church door in Coria, Spain, has a banderilla thrust in its' anus. Local 'Franciscan' nuns construct and sell these vile implements!

Complimentary to the cover photo, yet another goat is thrown from a Spanish church tower for sport - with full approval of the parish priest. After all, they're only animals and holy church has decreed that they have neither rights here nor a place hereafter!

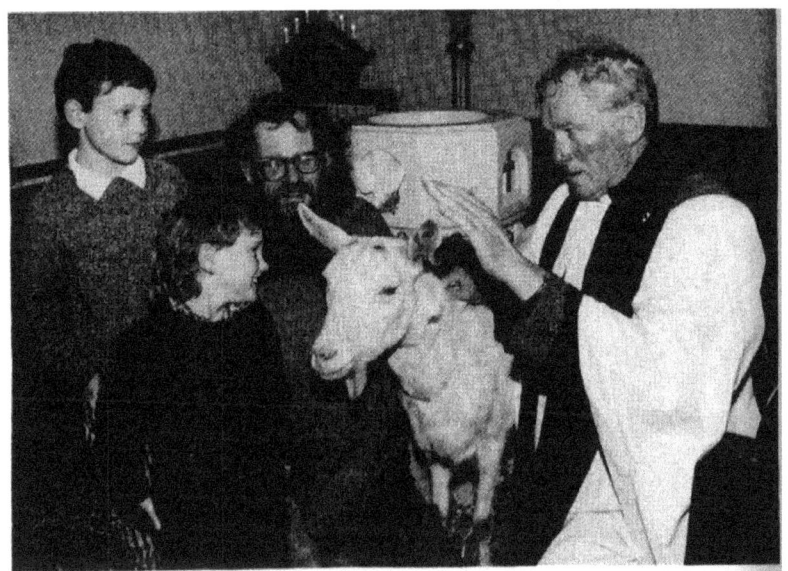

(Top) As befits real Christianity, this creature was treated with dignity. Receiving red carpet treatment - once the blessing service was over she began to chew a portion of it! Goats **will** be goats!

(Bottom) Sharing a service as guest to the gentle Catholic Dean Of Wiesbaden. The author and Dean bless a rescued cat. Whereas dogmas and creeds had kept us apart, dogs and cats brought us together!

(Top) The concern of German Christian animal activists for the helpless is superb. It would never have allowed world wars between us! Pastors Michael and Christa Blanke hold services in a big way!
(Bottom) Blake's words go: 'Little lamb who made thee; dost thou know who made thee?' This one certainly knew; and so does the pony!

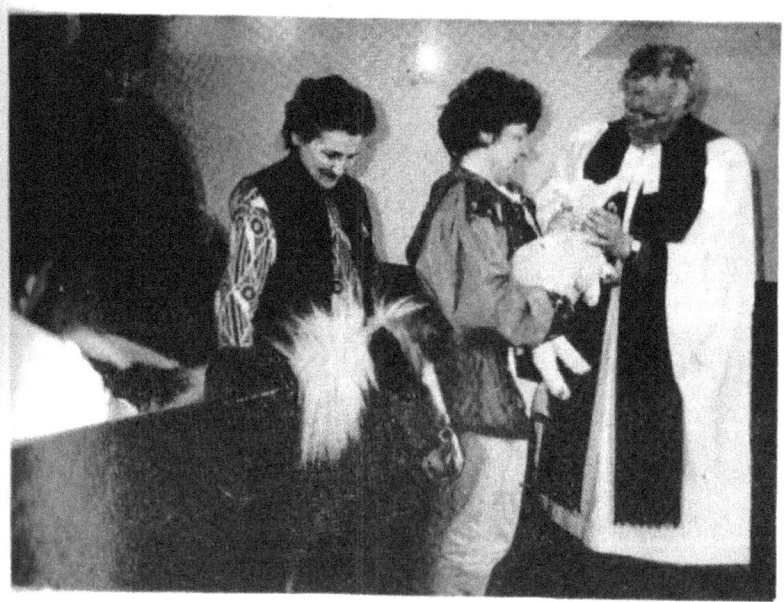

(Top) In 1982 representing the Anglican Society For The Welfare Of Animals – 'against the live export of animals'. Such an evil still persists. It will **not** go simply through diplomacy and courtesy!
(Bottom) In 1975 these hens – **rescued by godly animal liberators** – were simply 'skin and bone' (and not much skin!). Within 2 months this photo was taken in Milnsbridge vicarage garden, Huddersfield!

Reprehensible Practices

Centre illustrations within this book convey their own message to us. Some reflect a Denomination's theology and distorted morality. However, one needn't go to Spain! We have much cruelty in Christian Britain. There has been the barbaric crated veal unit which monks of the Dominican Order (founder of the 'Inquisition'!) at Storrington in West Sussex ran, until the end of 1988. This was despite extensive opposition from animal welfare groups such as Compassion in World Farming who fought a hard legal battle, only to lose it. But, thanks to the heightening public indignation the case aroused, the monks had little option but to terminate the unit. Their calves were tethered by a short chain from the neck while being kept in narrow crates. They were hardly able to lie down and unable to turn round. Exercise would hinder them from putting on weight with the minimum of food! They had previously been taken from their mothers only a short while after their birth – to spend the first six weeks of their short lives standing on wooden slats, within crates two feet wide and denied even straw for bedding. They were then, finally, loaded on to lorries for export; a frightful journey to France awaiting them.

Indeed, this abominable practice of live export of animals, to various far-off lands, is another account of the depth of depravity to which professed Christians will sink in order to receive 'fresh' meat on their plate.

The monks obviously were not troubled about such moral issues. As the victims were animals the matter is irrelevant. The trouble for them came from the stormy protests of animal activists as well as mounting public indignation which followed. 'How could assumed holy men do such things?' Although Roman Catholicism has up to recent years constantly suppressed the Scriptures lest the faithful become enlightened, the Bible being for centuries a banned book for the laity, Scriptural quotations are used when they serve an end; as when a journalist at one of these protests here was eagerly informed by a leading monk that Christ condoned their intensive rearing practice. He referred in one of the parables to the father who killed the 'fatted' calf for a prodigal son (Luke 15:23)! One need only to say that using such strange reasoning one could equally affirm, from using another parable in this way, that because a lord commended an unjust rogue, Christ condones unjust rogues too (Luke 16:8)!

The poorer Reillustrations of the nuns (the originals soon became unobtainable!) were taken at the battery unit at Badby near Daventry. The Sisters Of The Passion, during the last decade, were passionately engaged in their highly remunerative egg production business. Not only had the monks at Storrington been so obsessed with filthy lucre (1 Peter 5:2) as to violate government codes, having two feet narrow crates instead of a minimum three, but the nuns, similarly, were cramming five birds to a cage when the maximum stipulated was then four!

Protests had repeatedly been made by animal activist bodies – including that most worthy movement: the Roman denomination's own 'Catholic Study Circle for Animal Welfare'. After forcing an entry thirty members of the A.L.F. staged a sit in protest: a means of drawing public attention to the appalling conditions. One of them wrote later: 'Inside the shed we tried not to breathe too deeply because of the smell. We were all quite horrified to see the hens with red featherless necks. Horror turned to disgust when we found that there were five hens in a cage, and in some six. This was in cages measuring 14½x21½" and the birds averaged 4lbs in weight'.

A journalist's account summed up this particular demonstration in these words: "These non-violent protesters were ejected by the police. There springs to mind a precedent in which some doves were released from their cages and some money changers tables overturned".

Yes, apt words indeed! The most disconcerting fact is that this religious order guilty of such utter callousness was, and no doubt still is, the possessor of no less than ten acres of beautiful park land. This they use for contemplation; would that they might have contemplated grazing their hens upon it!

Later, at this same establishment, one was hardly surprised to learn of salmonella having broken out; and as a consequence, their evil trade has had to cease.

Across the water, during the same past decade, in 'God fearing' Ulster a Father John Conlon was receiving prominence at The Abbey Of Our Lady Of Bethlehem: a 'holy' establishment running a 300 head beef fattening farm with also 32,000 broiler hens. The cruelty of the broiler system is a story in itself. What gratified the monks was that even more revenue was to come their way through their ability to transform the massive quantities of slurry and manure into further profit.

The writer wishes to make it clear that the above instances quoted and illustrated are largely taken at random and equally typical of some others. At the same time, he in no way doubts the religious sincerity of so many who live out their days in the confines of religious orders. Monasteries and convents have been frequented by him and the inmates are, mostly, highly devoted to their vocations. The sad fact is that such lack of morality, or the limits of it, are but the outcome of a conditioning which is speciest. Yes, these 'religious' of our day are regrettably as obsessed by their rites, robes, rituals and repetitions as were the priests and pharisees who crucified Our Blessed Saviour. Add to this their fondness for titles and the resemblance becomes quite uncanny. (Matthew 6:7 and 23:4-10).

The cruelty that Christian civilisations inflict upon dumb creatures is not, however, to be confined to factory farms. It involves almost every marketable product sold in the corner shop or supermarket. The responsibility for this is linked with the abominable LD50 test which still has full governmental backing today, as it had with previous governments. This is hardly the publication for discussing 'in depth' the evils of such a practice: sufficient to say that a selection of animals are force fed a substance – anything from floor polish to oven cleaner – until fifty per cent of the poor creatures have died. The purpose being to assess the toxicity level poisonous enough within the substance to fatally poison half of them.

The whole process, of such experimentation is, of course absurd and dangerously misleading: what is poison to one species is often food to another. Rabbits, for example, can feed on deadly nightshade as well as on types of toadstools which are lethal to any humans. Animals even differ amongst themselves: penicillin kills guinea pigs but not mice. As for assessing toxicity levels via a death percentage, mortality well be the result of burning, haemorrhaging, choking, etc!

The abominable LD50 test is, in fact, no more than a cover up whereby the chemical and drug industries might save face in the event of legal action brought against them. They could then truthfully say that they had fulfilled the legal requirements stipulated by governmental and medical standards.

Yes indeed, a liaison that one perceives between the multi-million pound drug industry and the nation's final voice on health issues, hoodwinks the masses very well indeed. Alas for the traditional churches; as they are never far away, always ready to give their imprimatur and blessing to such a marriage. You scratch my back and I'll scratch yours!

The cosmetic industry is still riddled through with the torture of animals. Not only has the above test been put into practice by firms such as Boots (now selling a choice of cruelty-free items); but other tests, of which one must suffice, have equally been used:

The Draize test (named after its sadistic inventor!) clamps groups of rabbits into restraining devices whereby they are denied the ability to struggle while injurious and harmful substances are constantly dropped into their eyes. Rabbits are used as physiologically they are unable to cry! However, the test is quite absurd because the texture of a rabbit's eyes is different from that of a human. Consequently, saner companies use alternatives.

Such hideous and cruel practices as the LD50 and Draize tests have full governmental backing, and though a multitude of bishops sit in the House of Lords, never a voice of protest is raised on such matters by them. Martin Luther King once said, 'To passively condone an evil is to be as guilty as to perpetrate it.' Yes, there is blood on the hands of those who profess to be the spiritual and moral mouthpiece of our nation. Of course, not every animal welfare association will support the present writer in this contention. He well remembers criticising a panel containing an archbishop, a bishop, and other clergy. The chairman – then prominent in animal welfare – was not a little disturbed. The writer, complete in 'dog collar', was not allowed to address the panel further, even though the audience had given him a resounding ovation. There are, indeed, times when diplomacy amongst welfarists is better termed disgust!

There is exceeding cruelty due to the fur and skin industries. As a result of a demonstration concerning the former, and the newspaper publicity which followed it, a regular worshipper ceased to attend a church where the writer was a member of the staff. She was on close terms with a mink farm establishment! Indeed, **up to this very year**, the churches rather than condemn the fur industry, had truly condoned it. Clerics are still conspicuous, during public worship, strutting around flaunting their ermine hoods; and often before the assumed altar of God itself. The question of vanity rather than humility is hardly the subject of this book but the example of flaunting real furs most certainly is.

The laity of course are not immune from fault. What they've seen their clergy do, they imitate. 'Devout' communicants are still to be found, singing about their salvation with great gusto, while prominent in their animal furs. Though not as frequent as in the past (the work of the ALF is getting home!), we still see them approaching the Holy Table with great boldness to procure their heavenly food. Meanwhile, in the oven at home, their earthly food has been turned 'low'. The roast lamb or broiler fowl must not become a burnt offering!

'Hypocrites!' one might call these folk; and the title would be justifiable if they knew the cruelty their practices involved. Alas, most of them are no more than dupes within a society in which we all form a part. 'To whom much has been given of him much will be required', said our Lord. It is, surely then, with the leaders of our churches, and then with establishments of learning (such as the BMA and GMC) that the guilt must heavily rest!

Notoriously cruel sports are equally prevalent amongst animal loving Britons. The head family of the English Established Church is able to reconcile a position in the leading animal protection society with that of shooting wildlife! The typical country vicar of the past, joining in the hunt with the huntsmen, is not without successors today. His modern counterpart is simply cognisant of members of the community or congregation who are usually more sympathetic (thanks to animal rights protestors!) to the hunted rather than the hunter. So, the shrewd incumbent of English establishment – ever anxious to avoid rocking the boat – follows the example of his superiors. He sits on the fence to assess the side most are likely to favour, and then comes down to bless it!

Last but by no means least we have the fiendish practice of vivisection as perpetrated in medical and scientific research. Indeed, so heinous has the practice become that in many parts of the globe it is perfectly permissible for animals to be put into a vicelike contraption having had their voice boxes removed so that the agony of their cries is now only audible to their Maker. Such is again the depth of depravity, to which so-called medical and scientific men attached to hospitals, will stoop in order to ostensibly advance allopathic medicine. Not all of them are sadists. They are no more than peas out of the same pod; blueprints from the school of teaching, void through years of conditioning of any individuality or decisiveness of their own. Like rows of privates under a sergeant major they learn to obey rather than question if ever they are to ascend the ranks. In many respects they have much in common with hierarchic ecclesiastical structures, where total obedience to one's spiritual superiors is considered a mark of humility and a questioning attitude the mark of pride.

Within such medical and university complexes are often to be found chapels, not far distant from laboratories, where the vivisectors themselves may receive the Blessed Sacrament. They may also receive priestly absolution while they perpetrate their diabolical practices. The clerics who administer sacraments within these establishments do, indeed, have an affinity with some of the creatures of the labs! They also (to quote Isaiah's contempt of the same character type) are as 'Dumb dogs that cannot bark' (Isaiah 56:10).

Human nature changes little; education – as dished out in schools, colleges of further education and universities – has one thing in common: it makes little devils into big ones. It takes from the cruel caveman his club and replaces it with a fully equipped laboratory for all his requirements.

That vivisection, so forcefully denounced by Queen Victoria, and so bitterly condemned at first by converts to Roman Catholicism such as Cardinal Newman and Manning, should have spread to such astronomical proportions today is an appalling reflection on the character of the masses as well as the 'couldn't care less' attitude of those in positions of leadership. But then there is another subtler factor we do well to consider: vivisection is intensively used in return for funds collected by charities such as Cancer Research!

Down through the decades a similar message has constantly come across to the effect 'We are just about to arrive at a cure! The breakthrough is just around the corner now! – but we desperately need funds; will YOU help us?' What they do not mention – unless deeply pressed – are the massive assets they have acquired and the highly remunerative posts secured by their staff.

Cancer and Leukaemia research attract between them a million pounds a week in the UK alone. Indeed £21.5m alone is raised annually by advertising for legacies! Regrettably, people who would see through a beggar with a made-up story, or a woman begging money for the child she holds in the streets, are seemingly unable to see through what is – to the mind of the writer and many animal liberationists – **the number one charity con**. It has been said, and with much to support it, that in the USA there are more cancer researchers than patients with the disease itself!!

Vivisection covers very many areas of research as well as that of cancer. One of the most recent grotesque practices has been the work of Dr Robert White. His career has been involved in transplanting the heads of monkeys. He is an American and a very devout Roman Catholic! This learned man who has been doing such experiments, getting on for two decades, is the man who set up the bio-ethical committee at the Vatican to advise the present Pope on brain death, organ transplants, euthanasia and world health. He has met the Pope regularly being one of the 'four strong' committee to meet every year so as to advise Vatican staff on ethical medical issues!

After having transplanted numerous monkey heads, the above 'scientist' solemnly announced in 1977 that he was then ready to transplant a human head. So far as I know, he has found no takers-on! I wonder if it's because it's got around that it is neither possible to make cut nerves grow together or join the spinal cord to the head! The patient would probably always – if the operation succeeded – remain hospitalised. He would hardly be able to breathe without technical aids and would be void of speech. However, he **would** be able to suffer – as Dr White's monkeys did! None of them survived longer than seven days. 'Their faces became bloated, their tongues thickened, and their eyelids kept swelling until they closed down – forever' (quoted from Slaughter of the Innocent by Hans Ruesch).

Perhaps the most disturbing thing of all concerning the many head transplants taking place is that, through experimental techniques, isolated heads have become now increasingly normal; the brains appearing to function in a way which implied the retention of such sensibilities as one associates with the intact animal. And, indeed, if this is so then the sensations experienced by these minds must be unimaginably horrifying. It is not simply a situation of confusion, distress or shock, such as suffered by an appallingly mutilated but still living animal; it is a situation of artificially imposed amplification of pain, or other terrifying sensations, from which the natural relief mechanism has been disconnected.

'Under conditions of extreme pain, or mortal fear, an intact animal will faint or become comatose through loss of blood supply to the brain. But this release from pain and fear is not available to heads fed by a machine or donor. The pump goes on, regardless of the brain's sensations and whatever the level of pain.' (Slaughter of the Innocent by Hans Ruesch).

As a leading vivisector, Dr White from Ohio has had no qualms of conscience. The teaching of his church has saved him from any feelings of guilt or remorse. To a News on Sunday journalist of May 1989, he could affirm, "Animals in my judgements have no rights. The use of animals for medical experiments has no relevance in human theology."

That such an ecclesiastical structure of the Church of Rome should give its blessing to such diabolical practices as vivisection while at the same time denouncing poverty-stricken families for practising birth control speaks for itself. Did not the Good Shepherd say that every tree shall be known by its fruit (Matthew 7:15-20)! But please, just in case you think the writer is victimising Rome, he need only add that the present archbishop of York, the second in command of the Church of England, was openly jeered at! When Dr Habgood was enthroned at the Minster, loyal animal activists were chanting the words, and largely displaying them: 'HABGOOD THE VIVISECTOR'. Yes, a prelate who has criticised, via the media, members of top royalty for lax moral standards, and prime minister John Major for wrong ethical values, was for five years licensed as a practising vivisector. Indeed, he still supports the 'responsible' practice of it, though he has neither graduated in medicine nor veterinary medicine. Incidentally, and hardly surprisingly, he chooses to retain the present writer on a blacklist which he distributes twice a year to diocesan bishops in Britain!

Retributive Penalties

People, on the whole, are very short sighted. Within childhood they were largely taught to do good and to decline from doing evil. Somehow, on reaching adulthood they then expect good results from evil practices. Though they've grown in stature they have correspondingly shrunk in soul.

What once horrified them as children they stand unmoved by as adults. Is it to be wondered that cancer and other killer diseases astronomically soar as one increases torture on the defenceless in quest of a panacea? Are we who claim to be Christian, conned into believing that God will use our appalling immorality which we sow each day so as to reap a harvest of health and prosperity from it? The short sighted, cruel and callous – as well as the academics who suffer from tunnel vision – will not have even associated the reaping with the sowing; but God has shown us from Scripture itself (and in the pages of history if we care to read them) that those who sow to the wind will reap the whirlwind. (Hosea 8:7).

A godly mother will teach her children that no blessing can come from any foul deed. If vivisection is right then the mother is wrong. So is the teaching of the Good Book itself, and history no longer makes sense. Yes, indeed, so void of perception, or else lacking in insight, has our generation become that we condition ourselves to believe that by mutilating and torturing a vast part of God's creation, good will come to us. We actually believe in doing evil that good may abound (Romans 6:1).

The longer we involve ourselves in seeking medical cures along immoral paths the further astray we will find ourselves from the only path a moral God can bless. Man flaunts divine laws which the Creator has imposed on His universe. Man can never really break them; he merely rebels against them and they break him! As a consequence, killer diseases and iatrogenic illnesses unknown a few decades past, are spreading as quick as any prairie fire.

Would to God that we might get off this once assumed pleasurable merry-go-round, once viewed as a solace but now completely out of control and racing on to a horrid disaster for all it carries. If only people could dissociate themselves from a system which has so tightly ensnared; if only people could stop and listen and learn. They might then recollect words similar to those once offered to the writer when he was a young teenager; words offered by a wonderful mother and later by an aged printer: 'No lasting good will ever come from a mean deed. Mark my word son!

People are constantly seeing the sense of furthering conservation. They know that to constantly exploit even the inanimate world is to eventually exterminate ourselves. It is becoming increasingly obvious to them that the whole of life is interdependent. Unfortunately, some who do see the sense of such reasoning do not always consistently extend this to the animate conscious world that exists outside their own species. The humanitarians – for the sake of humanity alone - are seeing the sense of a vegetarian food policy which would result in enough food for every human mouth. They may well know, as do many animal activists, that it takes approximately ten tons of vegetarian protein to be converted into one ton of meat protein. One wonders how any philanthropist, knowledgeable of such facts could ever remain carnivorous!

The policy of sowing and reaping needs also to be considered in the light of sensitivity and its opposite: callousness. Most children usually possess a clear sensitivity towards helpless animals which hardened adults appear, regrettably only too eager to stifle or else to serve. Let the writer refer to two personal examples:

While visiting a delightful parishioner to discuss the growing need of Christians to remember animals in public prayer, he happened to mention recent instances involving a vivisector and his experiments for cancer research, when, quite out of the blue, the unexpected noise of heavy sobs was heard from a corner in the back of the room. The little lad who'd quietly slipped into the room possibly in childlike fashion to eavesdrop, had to identify himself. He could stay unnoticed no longer. "but how could they mummy; how could these horrid evil men do such a thing?" Then turning to the writer, he asked "Can you tell me James – just how they could be so evil?" This wonderful lad of ten knew that such evil could never be justified; so did the writer. To whitewash the barbarity by referring to the need of combatting disease for humans is a price young Matthew would never have accepted. He reminded the writer of a much earlier experience:

A much younger lad was crying bitterly while he carried a well-worn teddy bear in his arms. "What's the matter?" asked a stranger. The little lad lifted up the arm of his teddy. It was noticeable that a piece of the stuffing was protruding from the seam that had come apart. The truth of the matter was that the little lad had put two and two together and sensed that Teddy must be in pain and he was crying in sympathy with it! Well might Isaiah, visualising a restored Paradise inhabited by beasts and humans together, say, 'And a little child shall lead them' (Isaiah 11:6). With the passing of years man intellectually progresses while spiritually regresses! "Who is the greatest in the kingdom of Heaven? .... And Jesus set a little child into their midst" (Luke 9:47)!

One factor is sure: our educational systems are exceedingly dangerous. The writer has taught in a grammar school, lectured in colleges of further education and is on a board of education. He knows that the system as taught by the authorities and accepted by the parents is geared to encourage rivalry for self-centred ends. The religious and ethical factors are of little interest to most parents. How their child can out-do the neighbour's child is of far more relevance! It is more concerned with encouraging scholastic attainments for selfish ends than in implanting sensitivity as to how we treat those weaker than ourselves. It encourages the rat race while it lacks the compassion and sensitivity of such a rodent. It conditions people to be lopsided: to have a mind as bloated as a baseball while their soul becomes as shrivelled as a peanut. And its top specimens will be those who rule, influence and legislate. Heaven help us! The present system conditions children to become callous while it encourages dissection, later becomes a vivisector – and should the end product be that of a doctor, one factor will obviously be missing: sensitivity towards suffering. Yet the public at large wonder why 'lack of sensitivity towards patient's problems' is the number one criticism levelled towards GPs and their health centres. A Nation that expects those it conditioned to be callous as children to be caring as adults is a Nation sadly lacking in foresight.

The fruits of desensitisation had evolved but one rung lower during the notorious reign of the Third Reich. Adolf Hitler was one of those rare exceptions whose compassion for animals and consistent refusal to eat them did not soften his attitude towards the Jews. His henchmen were allowed to use the later as 'laboratory models' in place of animals. Of course, the vivisectors themselves would no doubt give these human models every bit as much consideration as they had previous animal models; they were largely men of character who had sworn on the Hippocratic oath! The only difference was that the law of the land which had protected humans from being used in such experiments was withdrawn. Medical researchers were at last free to do fully what they wanted so as to benefit the Master race. It must have been a vivisector's dream of Paradise; the only Paradise they'll ever witness! However, free to reveal their previously concealed sadism, it became manifest to mankind. The most excruciating suffering imaginable was perpetrated by them; and most seemed in their element to do it! Callousness had been superseded by calculated cruelty.

As touched on previously, sadistic tendencies do at times appear in children, yes and in the most sensitive ones! Unless such tendencies are checked then the disease rapidly spreads. Throughout one's life one is constantly coming across those whose character Freud termed 'anal, sadistic or paranoid'. Ruthless ruminative people, devious and scheming, though often masked by a surface geniality. But once they are in a role of a master and you their servant, then the mask is removed. Every school class contains them, every large office, shop or work room. The one you rub shoulders with in the local may appear delightfully kind and amiable, but get into a position of subservience to him and off comes the mask and the sadism is glaring at you. The only protection is your chief gaffer, your union, or your threat to move elsewhere. But once these things are denied to you – as they were to the Jews and as they are to the animals – you'll witness the true depth of depravity that lurks within his heart. Remember then that many a vivisector who is outwardly gentle, courteous and kind to you reveals a totally different nature towards the victims in the privacy of his laboratory. Although the fictional story was written when this most fiendish of medical practices was in its infancy, remember that 'Dr Jekyll and Mr Hyde' was one person by profession: a medical vivisector!

And now, thanks to the meddling of vivisectors, (affirm the N.A.V.S.) they have unleashed upon our communities the deadliest virus of our day: AIDS! Indeed, all over the USA during the sixties and seventies vivisectors were deliberately transmitting simian AIDS from animal to animal, species to species, laboratory to laboratory cruelly and irresponsibly watching it develop in its severity and speed of action. No attempt was made to contain the viruses. At this stage the human consequences of such work were unknown. It was not anticipated that retribution must surely follow, as night the day! In their vile laboratories they have manufactured a worse potion than the draught which turned a physician into a fiend. They are the fiends whose irresponsibility now results in thousands of harmless people undergoing a slow and wasting death – the type of disease they derived pleasure from analysing, and worked to actually increase, in laboratory models of a different species from theirs.

Bearing the above in mind, one becomes more than a little disgusted when supposed men of God seek to attribute AIDS to a divine retribution upon the homosexual community. Sexual promiscuity can certainly have its evils, of that the Bible is in no doubt; but clerics who condone vivisection while they condemn liaisons acceptable to consenting adults exhibit a morality on par with the pharisees: It sought to stone the adulteress and succeeded in crucifying the Messiah!

The Jewish treatment by Hitler's regime is, to our mind, totally barbaric and inexcusable. We need only to realise however that the culprits had been conditioned to view the rapidly spreading Jews in their midst as we have been conditioned to view a spread of rats in our midst! The former was viewed as an economic and social menace; the latter would be viewed by us as a health menace. When the health of a nation, of whatever kind, is sorely at risk and the assumed culprits are spotted, compassion goes out of the window and emotions that give impetus to action become hostile instead of holy. The victims are shown no mercy no matter how religious or otherwise their opponents claim to be. The same warfarin is put down!

The Nazis, of course, would hardly have treated their fellow countrymen in the way they did the Semites. An emotional bond would have forbidden it. Similarly, an emotional bond would forbid as from giving poison for vermin towards cuddly, friendly cats and dogs! Morally, people on the whole (mostly C of E because it's a religion which costs least) only seek to love and protect the things they like: and things include animals. When the pleasure from protecting such a thing wears off then the RSPCA kennels take over; or the creature is abandoned to the streets. Today there is little sense of duty taught. Emotions largely dictate. What you like you keep and what you don't, you throw away! It starts with a child's lack of responsibility to its pets and it culminates in an adult's irresponsibility towards one's partner. Marital love becomes no more secure than love for a rabbit until commanded to constantly feed it and clean the hutch. How the child treats an animal will largely influence the way it will as an adult treat a close friend or partner.

Our likes and dislikes, and how we react to them, results in the formation of character; and in this religious upbringing has had a large part to play. One need only say, to quote but one trouble spot, that if the children of Ulster had been taught by their churches about the Sermon on the Mount, the example of Jesus, or the tenderness of a St Francis, as they have the dogma and bigotry of Churchianity then things would be different. Their land would be a haven of refuge instead of a bloodbath. Both sides of the religious war have blood on their hands. They each sowed bigotry and hatred in decades past and they are now reaping it. Their desire to palm off responsibility on to secular ideologies today is quite futile. Indeed, the world is engulfed in battles; and, to be honest, more are caused by religious factions than political ones, though you can't always disentangle one from the other. In such a chaos relief often seems more forthcoming from Eastern Faiths than Western ones. We know that if all people were as loving, caring and sensitive to defenceless life as to refuse to kill it for food, then as a corollary all wars would have literally ceased which involved the taking of life! For most of us in the western spheres, we are too sensitive to kill the defenceless for food. We employ others to do the dirty work for us! This takes place in premises we would rather not know about. Hence, we build them largely out of sight, hoping that they will also be out of mind. We call these grotesque slaughter houses abattoirs; it helps to camouflage what goes on in them! Similarly, with the products of the same, we prefer to call bull 'beef' and pig 'pork. What hypocrites we really are! We're only deceiving ourselves as well as poisoning ourselves too: physically, as well as morally and spiritually.

If we are to usher in 'Paradise restored' and not merely sing 'Thy Kingdom come O God, Thy rule on earth begin', then a vegetarian diet (as prophesised for that Kingdom (Isaiah 65:25) is a very real way in working with our Risen Lord to actualise it. It is purely our task to prepare the way! As already touched upon it will benefit the starving humanity of man as well as beast. The alternative is that we continue to perpetrate the present flesh eating (carnivorous) practice. Financing others to murder on our behalf; and nowadays assimilating into our very life stream not only the fruits of intensive suffering through factory farm rearing, but also with it a mass of hormones, drugs and antibiotics! Yes, via the traditional English breakfast, people are consuming into their bodies the devastating fruits of

Britain's top health hazard. The poor animal injected with deadly drugs to produce hormone growth and forced to feed on drug-impregnated animal fodder ends up on the average plate for breakfast. And should illness overtake the consumer he is usually advised to consume yet more. The fruits of pain and poison are on the plate and paradoxically man eats it for health and wholeness!

Sooner or later (with a few merciful exceptions) the bill arrives (Romans 6:23a)! Cancer amongst heavy flesh eaters is one killer that is very high. But the high-pressure drug industry is still at hand to benefit; more poison in the form of chemotherapy is still at hand, plus a multitude more. The deadliest hazard of all works side by side with and through the profession that professes to heal and save! Who pays for all this vast empire? We do, the tax payer, and we have no freedom to opt out from financing what for moral and medical grounds we might choose to oppose. We are forced to finance the massive drug empire via allopathy as well as armaments! The horrors of animal torture involved in the latter would be another book in itself.

The side effects of drugs, as well as their direct results, would take up volumes. Thalidomide is the most well-known, but there are countless others equally as harmful even though they didn't result in the same wave of publicity. Iatrogenic diseases are coming up, or being discovered, like the growth of mushrooms. The writer himself had never experienced tinnitus until he was urged to use several brands of antibiotics as ear drops. Though unsuccessful in terminating the discharge the tinnitus increased. The discharge subsequently ceased through homeopathy; and the tinnitus with complementary hypnotherapy plus a change of lifestyle. What was previously an unbearable roar is hardly a ring! Yet the British Medical Association is, on the whole, far from favourably disposed towards the world of Alternative Medicine. With its marriage partner – the drug industry, it seeks to suppress all rivals, or else takes such therapies under its own umbrella and claims priority of right, to use afterwards!

Reactionary Protests

The leavening influence of Roman scholasticism has affected more than its own denomination. Though a Reformation threw out the many doctrinal inaccuracies of that church due to their irreconcilability with Scripture, and though many 'humanly' immoral practices amongst clerics, lay brothers and nuns had now been forbidden within Catholicism through its Council of Trent, the influence of Thomas Aquinas still lives on. Yes, and only to a lesser degree within the vast Protestant world.

It was generally accepted that animals had no such thing as an immortal soul. Consequently, although that reformation and cleansing of the churches face would soon be enhanced through the innovation of public hymn singing. Congregationalists, such as Isaac Watts (father of English hymnody) would give no place within hundreds of beautiful hymns for God's animal creation. And Methodism 'born in song' a century or so later would give no reference to praise for either bird or beast!

Aristotle lived on in Aquinas and Rome still lives on in the Reformed! It is all a contrast to the biblical negativism of the book of Ecclesiastes on the one hand (3:19 & 20) and thankfully to the biblical positivism of the book of psalms on the other (Psalm 104:29 & 30)! But thanks to God, this exclusion of other creatures from hymnal as well as Heaven is now being corrected. The present writer compiled such a work in 1988 and, incidentally, it was not the first. The credit for that must go to a past 'Society of United Prayer for Animals' which published a booklet in the 1960s under the chairmanship of one of those freelance yet quite remarkable bishops: a Right Reverend T Paget King.

The appalling paradox is that though life beyond the grave was considered exclusive to man, and animals had no rights whatsoever, the western church has considered them in the past to be accountable for their actions. (This was at a time when their groans under the vivisector were considered synonymous with the creaking sound of an inanimate wheel revolving on its axis!) Consequently, ecclesiastical courts were set up in which dumb creatures were brought into the dock for trial.

Perhaps the only thing that existed in the favour of these dumb beasts was that a counsel could act on their behalf! The poor creature, be it dog, pig, donkey, bull or other animal, would stand before the full assembled court – culminating in the judge then donning his black cap when considered necessary. In animal loving Britain this, hard to believe, practice persisted up to as late as 1771 when a dog was put on trial in Chichester.

Thanks, however, to the later influence of non-clerical Quakerism which originated in Britain, and to the even later emergence – its Methodism, things began to slowly improve for the animal kingdom. Consistently, those in whom the Holy Spirit shone, were witness to the poor dumb creation as well as to the whole callous nation. The saintly John Wesley – denounced and deprived by the Church of England – was a vegetarian as well as a practitioner in the alternative medicine of his day. Need one be surprised that he was healthily active to the ripe old age of ninety-two!

This little man from Epworth, Lincolnshire, proclaimed a gospel which he refused to limit to any supposed elect of men. He considered the whole world his parish. Need one wonder that in writing of the animal creation he could say: "Something better remains after death for these poor creatures also." Yes, this was heresy to the establishment but it was simply a reflection of his spiritual depth, indeed, his scriptural depth also.

Around this period two much lesser-known clergymen produced truly monumental works for their day. One was the Reverend Richard Dean who published in 1768 'An Essay on the Future Life of Brute Creatures'! Yes, here and there, in a society where the average country figure of the Church of England indulged in cruel sports, isolated voices of protest would be heard; scattered in some remote spots a clerical voice for the defenceless beasts would be raised.

Indeed, two years after Dean's essay a most monumental work was published for which the writer was awarded a doctorate in divinity from Aberdeen. He was the Revd Humphry Primatt who compiled his thesis in retirement at Kingston upon Thames. This was before vivisection had been thought of. The appalling fact is that the same part of Aberdeen university today is notorious for animal experimentation (see photo of demo outside of it!).

Yes, and within this same latter half of the eighteenth century and beginning of the nineteenth there were non-clerical carers too. One of the latter was Erskine of Les Trommel who, as a leading lawyer rose to become Lord

Chancellor. It is recorded of him that on rebuking a man for beating his horse he received an abusive reply stating "I can certainly do what I want with my own". "Yes, so can I" replied Erskine – "This stick in my hand is my own!" and he there and then administered a non-judicial thrashing!

Another influential humanitarian of the same era was that man of the Bar, Richard Martin who later became MP for Galway. Because of his stand against animal exploitation George IV nicknamed him 'Humanity Dick'! Yes, and another contemporary was William Wilberforce whose childhood association with the Methodist movement no doubt encouraged his later all-embracing compassion.

Regrettably, little did the above activists realise that across the water in Europe a contemporary creature was studying medicine whose future would involve experiments of torture that they, themselves, could never have envisaged. He was Claude Bernard, yet to be discussed.

Meanwhile, within Britain, a group of people concerned for the plight of the animals gathered for an evening meeting in 1824. It was within a fashionable part of London's west end. Their meeting had been convened by an unobtrusive and humble cleric who had chosen for himself to work in London's east end! This vicar was the Reverend Arthur Broome, and the outcome of that meeting was the formation of an animal welfare society. It was later to be known as the RSPCA! Broome was to resign his post as Vicar of St Mary's Bromley, so as to give the whole of his life as a spokesman and fighter for the dumb creation. However, debts soon arose for which the poor fellow was thrust into prison. He may well have spent a lengthy stay in a primitive cell but for the intervention of a philanthropic Jew and a humanitarian lawyer who came to his rescue, paying his debts and securing his release.

However, as in the history of Christendom, so similarly within the animal cause, an early zeal and fervour often diminishes and is followed by a spirit of compromise with opposing forces. As for those who remain staunch, they have a tendency to break away and remain unmoved. The result is faction as one disowns the other. The history of Christianity and of Denominations within it, are a prime example here. We are consequently hardly surprised to witness similar upheavals within the animal protection movement. Sadly, people fail to realise that far more harm can be done to both movements through disruption within the ranks than from disturbances outside them. Interference from within results in cracks which often becomes chasms. Opposition from forces without merely helps to strengthen and consolidate the movement within!

Consciousness of a common foe without brought about political consolidation during the past war with Germany; animal activist and welfare movements need to realise that our foe is one! This would help them to realise that our apparent differences are more often than not complimentary rather than contradictory ways of opposing the same evils. It is not surprising, therefore, to learn that a split in the ranks between the militants and moderates occurred way back at the beginning of the animal caring movement, amongst the supporters of the Revd Arthur Broome.

Meanwhile, as early animal activists began to squabble within, across in the continent animal cruelty was spreading with tentacles soon to be felt in Britain. Vivisection – the dissection of live and usually conscious animals – with subtlety referred to by its originator as 'experimental physiology' is basically attributed to Francoise Megandie; and this, most forcefully by his protégé: Claude Bernard, a man who has been frequently referred to as 'father of modern medicine'. Such a prize pupil – for lack of sensitivity was to surely be on par with Descartes 'father of modern philosophy'! Indeed, both characters in their day were acknowledged as good Catholics, and Claude Bernard had studied at a Jesuit foundation. The philosopher had dogmatically affirmed that animals were void of all feeling and that their screams were no more conscious than the perpetual creaking of the revolving spit, and the vivisector was to experiment on fully conscious animals as if this were indisputably the case.

The place in which this vile practice (referred to by Mahatma Gandhi as 'the blackest of all crimes') began was within a small laboratory attached to the College-de-France in Paris. Though they nicknamed it the 'drab kitchen' it was the first laboratory of its kind to be officially authorised and funded by a supposedly learned institution; and it was in reality nothing less than a diabolic torture chamber. Nevertheless the founder of experimental physiology, with his prize pupil Bernard, allowed audiences to attend many of his lectures. And apart from medical students and doctors there would frequently be an assortment of women, priests and monks!

Yes, the establishment had been given a veneer of respectability through a gloating, depraved clerical observation. No wonder the fiendish practice was to spread elsewhere with a similar establishment soon to raise its ugly head within Italy itself! But then, before a few decades were out, its diabolical tentacles had contaminated countries as puritanical as Presbyterian Scotland. This was through the depraved influence of a notorious Professor John Reid of St Andrews.

Renowned and sensitive British medical men, such as Sir Charles Bell and the famous John Elliotson (a brilliant hypnotherapist before that name was coined!), were extremely disturbed over what was happening. However, such protests as they made were too solitary to stem this tide of evil that was becoming a torrent. Sir Charles's revulsion had been due to having visited one of Megandie's later establishments where – to try and confirm to him and others the location of those roots of nerves which leave the spinal cord in pairs, and their respective functions – Megandie had sacrificed no less than four thousand dogs.

The process of opening up to view and tampering with such a nervous system in a fully conscious creature, was an expression of the depth of depravity to which the first 'experimental physiologist' had sunk. Is it to be wondered that a common view expressed by animal activists is this: 'If the devil exists in the mind of an animal he appears in the form of a man: a vivisector!' Yes 'If hell exists, it's not a pit but a lab!' Dr Samuel Johnson was moved to write within The Idler of 1758: "It is time that a universal resentment should arise against these horrid operations which tend to have hardened the heart, making the physicians more dreadful than the very gout or the stone!".

This chapter is primarily about 'reaction'. It is therefore worthy of comment that Claude Bernard's wife eventually left him; and after he died, much to their credit, she and his daughter actually started an animal welfare movement. I wonder if they were the very first anti-vivisection group! Action however, that was organised rather than solitary or spasmodic was later formulated against this scourge of Europe, and it occurred most appropriately within Florence the city of the martyred Savanarola who had opposed Papal corruption as far back as 1498. The reformer this time, however, was a lady, and what is more she was Irish by upbringing and a devout humanitarian with influence. She was a close relative of the Anglican archbishop. Coming from the same emerald isle she was to prove as strong a spokesman for the animal cause as her countryman Humanity Dick! This lady was to come into close proximity with an American who confirmed the reality of this newly assumed science: 'experimental physiology'. She learned of how it had actually taken root within Florence itself.

The year was 1863. The above lady was Frances Cobbe and as a devout Christian she had been attending to a dying minister named Theodore Parker. This cleric's physician was an American called Appleton, and he it was who confirmed to her in much distress the truth of a rumour they'd both heard: in connection with a certain Professor Sciff a laboratory existed for the purpose of physiological experiments. The shrieks and groans that came from it were undoubtedly real. It was not a horrid nightmare but stark reality which confronted them. There and then, Frances swore to do something about it; and this led to the enactment of a memorial to which no less than 783 signatures were appended. The publicity that followed resulted in public indignation and support throughout the city, and the guilty professor found it advisable to move away. Indeed, he chose Calvanistic Geneva. There the current theology implied that, apart from a chosen and decreed elect of humanity the sovereign God had no time in eternity for either man or beast. Consequently, the professor seems to have been left unmolested there!

In the prevailing warfare between good and evil the latter seemed to have got control. The devil knows his own. Need one wonder then that the ex-conspirator, Napoleon the third, should have come forward to finance for Claude Bernard a second laboratory in place of his existing 'drab kitchen'! As for Protestantism with its Calvinists and their limited elect of humanity and Romanism which denied emphatically and dogmatically all rights towards the brute creation, one is hardly surprised that things degenerated so rapidly. The moral mouthpiece for nations, the Christian Church, not only condoned vivisection but actually stood forcefully in the way of humanitarians who sought to oppose it.

In the middle of the last century when a Society for the Protection of Cruelty to Animals was desperately needed and about to be established within the imperial city itself the Pope stepped forward to forbid it: "The establishment of such .... Would imply that human beings have duties towards animals" he said. Need one wonder that the moral rot has so rapidly spread throughout the Latin world! But then, who are we to condemn, when within what foreigners call 'Animal loving Britain' today, an average of one animal every ten seconds dies at the hands of vivisectors?

Within twelve years from that first organised protest in Florence, Frances Cobbe had not only transferred her roots to Britain, but with the help of humanitarians as noble as the great Shaftesbury she had established the first large anti-vivisection society of its kind, the N.A.V.S. This was of course as late as 1875. But, again, as touched upon previously, the friction that exists between the radicals and those who seek reform by compromise would shortly create a split within her ranks. Frances had no time for those who worked via diplomacy and compromise; she was too much a revolutionary for that. Unable to inspire as much zeal in her followers as she herself possessed, she - rather than being held back – chose to break away, but only to create a much more militant movement: the BUAV (British Union for the Abolition of Vivisection). Thankfully, with the passing of the years, her first creation began to amend its ways and it too stands before us today as abolitionist.

Indeed, an offshoot of the NAVS was the Scottish Society for the Prevention of Vivisection, renamed Advocates For Animals. Through much diplomacy it got animal welfare into the political arena (and has similarly sought to get the same into the pulpit!). Indeed, a similar charity – as far as educational work is concerned – is the Animals' Vigilantes – of which the writer is a patron. Under the guidance of its dedicated founder Ted Cox, it has held church services for animal blessing since 1954. Animal vigilantes is highly represented by those in the theatrical profession whose concern for the animal creation could put the whole church to utter shame!

CIWF (Compassion in World Farming) – the work of an ex-farmer, is equally worthy of mention. It has done considerably good work for the cause both educationally and practically. Crusade Against All Cruelty to Animals, recently renamed 'Earthkind' has given past space to Christian leaders – not least, publishing Canon Hammerton's wonderful book: 'Kingdom of Neighbours'.

The organisations in the above paragraph, though not church affiliated, are most certainly Christian in outlook and activity; as is that most militant and vociferous of Scottish groups: Animal Concern (Scotland)'! And indeed, if the pen is truly mightier than the sword we can be grateful for the likes of a Rebecca Hall and her recent venture 'Writers Against Experiments On Animals'!

Space does not permit mention of other organisations. Some are worldwide, American or European – like those based in Germany and close to the writer's own heart!

The least reactionary movements have frequently worked through allopathic medicine, as well as through the law as it stands. This has often been via funds which finance 'research scientist' who are forbidden to use animals. Such charities are the Lord Dowding Fund and the Humane Research Trust. Thousands of animals have undoubtedly been spared because much fund raising has been spent on purchasing non-animal scientific methods.

Animal activists, who would destroy every vivisector's laboratory in order to liberate the animals are, on the whole, the most gentle, compassionate and caring of people. Animal Aid was founded by a wonderful lady who was a doer rather than a debater, and the Animal Liberation Front has done more to terrify the perpetrators of animal torture, without harming them, than all the other societies put together. Yes, as in church circles, so throughout the animal cause, valuable energy can be dissipated turning over the mechanism of countless bureaucracy and committees, which would be far better spent on direct intervention!

It might be that occasional animal activists have, like Barrabas, done more harm for the cause than good! However, when such liberationists defiantly flout the laws of a crooked state so as to obey those of a higher morality, they are in good company. My Lord and Redeemer did precisely that! They who put the sanctity of life before the security of property are people we need not fear. Let us rather beware of any regime that does the contrary: exacting heavy sentences on those who damage property and lenient sentences on sadists and muggers!

The law is indeed an ass, and so are the many judges who are supposed to be the epitomes of impartiality. Not a few of the latter who may remain remarkably cool and non-emotional while assessing an unprovoked rape charge become highly strung when guarded property is damaged or entered. Consequently, many sensitive activists have undergone severely harsh prison sentences through trying to rescue defenceless creatures from diabolical torture. And does the Christian church come to their aid? Not one bit. My experience is that she wouldn't as much raise one finger unless it were to criticise them.

A delightful teenager once known to the writer, served a harsh sentence for a raid which caused damage to a laboratory building. She was visited by a typical church 'do-gooder'. "Why don't you give your heart to Jesus?" asked her visitor. "I did it once, and since then life has been fab and whatever I've prayed for I've got!" Well, my friend Debbie was too nice a young lady to be bribed by such self-motivated jargon. And who with any depth of compassion could ever have blamed her!

Not all Christians, however, are as shallow as those who flaunt their colours most. A few animal-caring movements, Christian based, have sprung up over the last century and the Revd Arthur Broome has had occasional clerics to spur on the kind of work he so faithfully began. Indeed, the NAVS had amongst its early members churchmen as renowned as those two converts to Catholicism, Cardinals Newman and Manning! The former had made it clear: 'Cruelty to animals is as if we did not love God!' Sad indeed, that this denomination to which they turned – and for which they'd received the cardinal's hat in attempting to bring the Church of England into subjection to Rome – did not share such humanitarian views.

Though a more recent setback for catholic animal carers was, undoubtedly, when Pope Paul VI gave his endorsement of vivisection, **this past year 1993** has shocked us all! The new Catechism of the Catholic Church spells it unequivocally: "Medical and scientific work on animals, if they remain within reasonable limits, are morally acceptable since they contribute to caring for or saving human lives". The fact is, they don't!

A rebuff indeed for such a worthy and highly commendable society as the Catholic Study Circle for Animal Welfare established in the early 1930s! Against many odds this faithful circle battles along encouraging the St Francis's spirit within its own denomination; and one thing is indisputable:

their publication 'The Ark' is a pleasure to read. Of the animal pressure groups, church based, none can be more worthy of our prayers than this catholic study circle for animal welfare!

It was in 1934 that a 'Society for United Prayer for Animals' was established amongst a loose unorthodox group, and very helpful literature was circulated by them to the mainstream churches – including a collection of hymns (which I've already touched upon) along with prayers and litanies relevant to the animal kingdom.

And then – not to leave the establishment out! In 1970 the Church of England decided to do something about the cause. The outcome was the formation of the Anglican Society for the Welfare of Animals. Indeed, the spirit of ecumenism (of Christian denominations working together) has also resulted in the setting up of the Christian Consultative Council for Animal Welfare (of which the writer was an adviser, when less militant!). The balanced militancy and tactful diplomacy of May Tripp, a conservative evangelical of Leeds, has resulted in the formation of Animal Christian Concern, responsible for animal remembrance services being held in some top English cathedrals and abbeys. And now, thanks to two dedicated vegetarians of a liberal theological slant, Peggy Murray and Anna Partington, their work of 'Custodians' is emphasising the need for God's people to be vegetarian; and surely not before time! (Isaiah 66:3)

Frequently, it is these small groups that are doing the vital spade work. Larger groups – rightly or wrongly – have received criticism for sitting pretty, taking large salaries, hoarding the funds, or distributing with flippance!

We have a lady at Ellon, near Aberdeen, struggling to feed rescued monkeys; Tony and Vicky Moore, existing on a pittance while they expose, through the media sadistic sports in Spain and elsewhere. A young lady, until recently – on a Scottish island caring for strays *(sic)*. Such people, along with countless others running sanctuaries or fundraising for them, are Christ's 'salt of the earth'. For them the cause is not sitting back philosophising in affluence; neither is it compromising in convivial comfort; it's often struggling hand to mouth in wellies and blizzards.

We have an association of 'Doctors in Britain Against Animal Experiments'. There would be insufficient response for a similar Clergy association, but Christians Against Animal Cruelty is being launched by the writer later this year. Meanwhile, the dream of that superb journalist, Dr Vernon Coleman for 2000 is to be the year by which all organised animal cruelty must have ceased, is surely the dream we should all – religious or otherwise – be seeking to actualise!

Remedies Procurable

Down through the centuries religion has repeatedly divorced itself from righteousness. It has preferred to get so absorbed by rituals and regulations as to ignore it or, at best, put it into a subservient place. Because of this, Christendom has frequently failed man as well as beast. Corruption has spread while morality has been stifled and suppressed. Inquisitions which give absolute vent for sadistic clergy went hand in hand with pomp and ceremony, while the voice of the lone prophet became their next victim. Then, at a later age the laws of Leviticus were wrenched out of context so as to justify the practices of perverted witch hunters, supposing to purge a Puritan populace from the powers of darkness. But the pretext, whether it was a Catholic inquisition or a Protestant witch hunt, has been that of justifiable necessity to perpetuate the health of the populace at large. The 'professed' unpleasantness of the tasks was assumed a necessity as 'the end justified the means'! The masses were so conditioned and hoodwinked that they believed it all! Is not this an analogy of our present condition?

The public have been conned into believing that vivisection serves a very necessary end, the health of the nation! If horrifying diseases are to be conquered then sacrifice and suffering of the defenceless is considered an indispensable necessity. That the practice is indispensable is as much the view of the gullible masses as was the indoctrinated conviction of past Christians that people had to be stretched on a rack, their nails pulled out one by one, or that they be slowly burned alive so that the demons infesting the area be forever destroyed. Sadism has always had a marvellous way of masking its motives with a respectable veneer, and though many vivisectors are no doubt little more than dupes to a system, others are no less innocent than were those religious inquisitors or confessors of 'holy' church!

Indeed, that those dabbling in dark arts during the week - behind hidden doors – should appear at Mass or Matins on a Sunday is of no consequence whatsoever. Some may even be given to active charitable works as well – a way of seeking to wash away the defilement that can never be renewed; or a means of seeking to convey to an unperceptive public that there is nothing shady about their character at all. Such rituals – often, indeed, psychological obsessions – are but the outworkings of a dark and sinister neurosis from which they are unable to free themselves! Their outer morality, if one could call it that, may equally be no more than a desire to deaden a bad conscience and secure for them a period of peace. It could be akin to the practices of Ivan the Terrible who 'retired sometimes for weeks together to a monastery .... rang the bell for matins himself at three in the morning .... read, prayed and chanted with such fervour that the marks of his prostrations remained on his forehead. In the intervals he went to the dungeons under the monastery to see with his own eyes his prisoners tortured and always returned, it was observed, with a face beaming with delight!'

Perhaps the above analogy is rather harsh for a student who is largely coerced into practices others do, and which he is expected to fall in with, you might think; and you are possibly right! Perhaps the practice of vivisection hasn't persisted long enough to fan the flames of a dormant sadism. At such an early stage the medical student is, more likely than not, a duplicate of an educational system which turns out medics in one quarter as it does clerics in another. Yes, as peas from a common pod! Is it not a system of training which demands that superiors be revered as bordering on gods?

On the other hand, the world of alternative medicine lives and nurtures itself in a completely different soil as, indeed, does the world of the freelance evangelist, or the late Gladys Aylewards from the ecclesiastical clone and denominational duplicate. Advancement in a system comes by conformity to it along the lines it stipulates. The high priests of medicine share a similar awe to those of the church. Indeed, one might be excused for viewing them as buddies sharing a similar prestige and disturbed by similar rivals. Consequently, they are not averse at times to scratching each other's backs!

The only publication the writer has come across which is totally opposed to the overall advancement of Alternative Medicine (anything from Bach flower remedies to Bate's eye therapy!) is a work of 221 pages: "Understanding Alternative Medicine". The book receives not only a foreword by a general medical practitioner but a preface by the ex Anglican bishop of Glasgow who is now an assistant bishop of Wakefield! Practices such as hypnotherapy (of which the writer is a bona fide practitioner), homeopathy, herbalism, acupuncture and acupressure are all attributed to the occult and therefore of demonic origin. As for the evils and side effects of conventional drugs; the way the allopathic medical world thrusts them on to the populace at large, and as for the way they are diabolically and misleadingly tried out on animals, there is no criticism whatever!

The populace has far less to fear from alternative forms of medication; they have been used for a long time and are well tried and tested without the use of animals.

Alternative medicine is not only humane, it is also natural and usually safe. It is consistent with the Scriptures which tell of how the leaves of the trees will be for the healing of the nations (Revelations 22:2). Its other methods often have a similar scriptural affinity (Exodus 15:25); while yet another is also reminiscent of the first instance of painless delivery, though on this occasion just to start things off a male is chosen (Genesis 2:21)! Yes, and the more conventional mouth to mouth resuscitation (2 Kings 4:34), music therapy (1 Samuel 16:23) and the power of positive thought and healing (John 2:10 & Luke 17:14) are all justifiable therapies from the Christian's book of books. But, an allopathy – while it continues to reply on and perpetuate vivisection, and lay such high emphasis on synthetic drugs – no way! I don't think 'the beloved physician' would have approved (Colossians 4:14). As for the Divine physician; most certainly not! If clerics had spent as much time studying and applying the Scriptures, as they have commentaries and dead works of theology; and if those in the pew had spent as much time reading and applying Scripture as they have evangelistic titbits or lives of the saints, then the Christian population would be much healthier in every respect.

But now, in all fairness, I must give a word to the animal welfare and rightist movements. For they need to realise that just as in the whole of the British army there are a whole host of regiments whose methods and approaches vary considerably in attacking the same enemy, so, similarly, is the situation within the animal cause. Difference in strategy is not necessarily a bad thing just as union is not always strength. Indeed, the marriage of two sickly people never makes a healthy marriage! Within our century many Christian denominations, due to numerical loss, have come together to witness to the world that they are one. But as they really have little worthwhile to offer, the masses remain unconcerned. Today's animal activist and welfare associations could learn a great deal from this.

There is, on the contrary, a unity in diversity which is healthful and life imparting. One might see a Christian manifestation of this when those who choose to worship in different ways come together on specific occasions, as an act of witness that they are all seeking the same goal, and merely approaching it through complimentary channels. After all. The church is a body – the body of Christ and it's only a living spirit which keeps any body intact and free from decay. Indeed, the most offensive periods in church history have been those when the divine organism has been interpreted as an organisation to be held together by a hierarchic structure superimposed by man! Only those who possess the Spirit of Christ are part of His mystical body – the Church. Manmade dogmas supported by Catholic inquisitions or Protestant witch hunts, can only help to mummify a corpse which has no doubt already begun to decompose, and its stench has remained on the past pages of ecclesiastical history. God forbid that a similar evolution should ever mar the great cause towards animal liberation and those differing regiments (or denominations within it) which are all a vital part of its life force!

From a contrasting aspect it needs to be equally stressed: Let animal caring Church folk who derive blessing from united, ecumenical gatherings avail themselves of attending United animal demonstrations! They will learn more appropriately of what it is to walk behind a real cross rather than one of polished brass. Indeed, if all Christians who finance movements for animal concern would only turn up to support such demonstrations, then the battle would be more than half won. The truth is that while Christians confine the expression of their faith to a creed recited within four walls of a musty building, they equally often confine the expressions of their animal concern to the annual subscriptions of a society! These people are missing a great deal. Indeed, in entering the animal activist or welfare world one becomes part of a worldwide family which cares, and it's sad that so many hardly ever meet their brothers and sisters of varying temperament and outlook. Indeed, if I were not already married, I would have no need of a lonely-hearts group. I have always found amongst animal activists

ANIMALS PORTRAY JESUS CHRIST IN THE COVENANT WITH ABRAHAM: Genesis 15:9. Three animals are used, each is a 'willing servant of man' and each is to be three years of age; the same as the length of Jesus' ministry.

ANIMALS ARE FED BY GOD: Job 38:41, Psalm 104:10-30, 145:16 & Matthew 6:26.

ANIMALS ARE OF GREAT WORTH TO GOD: Luke 12:6, Job 39 (entire chapter)

CREATED BY JESUS CHRIST, ANIMALS ARE INCLUDED IN THE TOTAL SCOPE OF THE REDEMPTION: Psalm 36:6, Acts 3:21, Romans 8:18-25, 1 Corinthians 15:16-28, Colossians 1:15-17, James 1:18 (note: 'of His creatures'), & Revelation 4:11 &22:3 (in Psalm 36:6. 'preservest' – salvation).

ANIMALS ARE SEEN IN HEAVEN, PRAISING GOD: Revelations 5:13 – the word 'heaven' is the Greek Ouranos. The same word as used by Paul in 2 Corinthians 12:2. As for praising God, see also Isaiah 43:20, Psalm 150:6 (remember the 'breath of life'!) & Psalm 148 (entire).

ANIMALS ARE TREATED WELL BY BELIEVING PEOPLE: Proverbs 12:10. The word 'regardeth' means to have complete understanding and knowledge of something, or to know completely. The word 'life' is the word nephesh. Taken literally: Have skilful knowledge of the soul of your animal.

ANIMALS ARE CLEARLY PRESENT IN THE KINGDOM OF JESUS' REIGN ON EARTH: Isaiah 11:6-10, 65:17-25 & Hosea 2:18.

ANIMALS WERE GIVEN TO MAN AS COMPANIONS, HELPERS AND FRIENDS: Genesis 2:18-19.

ANIMALS ARE USED BY GOD TO DESCRIBE HIS CHARACTERISTICS TO US: Deuteronomy 32:11-12, Ruth 2:12, Psalm 17:8, 36:7, 57:1, 63:7, & 91:4, Isaiah 31:4, Hosea 11:10, 13:4-8, Amos 3:8, Matthew 23:37, Luke 13:34, Revelation 5:5-6.

Postscript

Clergy, congregations, and individual Christians, are constantly asked by registered 'charities' to raise funds for them. That any lover of the Good Shepherd should buy a flag, accept - pass round or display - a collecting box, arrange a collection in lieu of flowers, or leave a legacy for any cause which perpetrates vivisection must be a matter of individual conscience. BUT, let it be affirmed, those who support this outmoded research have blood on their hands!

Yes, regardless of how emotive or personal the plea from high-pressure charities; or how disturbing the 'tear jerking' methods that might be used; to animal protectors such as the writer, vivisection remains morally vile and not unnaturally, scientifically dangerous. But then; how could it be otherwise if a good God is behind the universe? None other than the Good Shepherd Himself! And if, in previous words quoted from Martin Luther King, 'to condone evil is to be as guilty as to perpetrate it'; how much more if we actually volunteer to finance it?

Thankfully – because of what animal rights raids have uncovered – there is a growing repugnance from the public towards animal experimentation. Educationally, it is no longer necessary to either dissect or vivisect in order to qualify in allopathic and veterinary professions. Sad, indeed, that while many medical and veterinary students are taking a moral and scientific against that this scourge that others – who are usually least knowledgeable about sensitivity and pain! – should be given freedom to execute such vile and horrific work.

The writer can assure you, from personal contact as well as via audio and video tapes, that what he has written is true. It is **NOT the obsessed overt sentimentalism of a pet loving cleric**. In fact, for ten years the writer has never possessed a pet!

What most animal activists have written as well as wrought, practised as well as preached, has had affinity with humble prophets and reformers of old. As already mentioned, they dared to challenge priests who despised righteousness while repeating ritual; and to denounce pharisees who preached purity but were perniciously perverse. Those prophets were defenders of the defenceless and spokesmen for the suppressed. Indeed, their fearlessness was the outcome of their fidelity (Proverbs 28:1). Some day their Good Shepherd may call **us** before His judgement seat, to separate into two categories (Matthew 25:34-46). Many a charismatic bishop could be there (Matthew 7:22)! Yes, many a regular communicant also (Luke 13:25-30)! To many of these used to calling Him 'Lord', he will say: "Depart from me, I never knew you!". But to many an animal liberationist - or carer on a windswept island, whose occasional reference to God might have been far from reverent! – I think I can hear Him say: "Come ye blessed of my Father, receive the Kingdom prepared for you". And they will say "But who are you Lord? We never worked for you!" Then with a searching look that penetrates the very heart, this Good Shepherd will say: "In that you did it to the least of these my creatures, you have done it to me". Yes, there will be weeping and gnashing of teeth when many clerics bearing crooks, and aligned in soft raiment, are turned away from the gates of the heavenly Jerusalem; and many a balaclavad activist is ushered in.

Creator of the sky and sea;
Of tiger, monkey, fish and bee.
Lord God of all that lives I dare;
To offer up my humble prayer.
I've woken from my fitful sleep,
With heavy heart and sorrow deep.
I dreamed of days when I was free,
And played and gambolled in the trees.

Alone imprisoned in this cage,
I try to calm my fear and rage.
How can I face another day
Of being tortured in this way?
Soon they'll come for me again,
And take me to their place of pain.
Please tell me Lord for I don't know,
Why do these people hate me so?

They've cut my vocal cords and tied
A heavy bandage round my eyes
I cannot see, I cannot scream,
This all seems like a fearful dream.
Twas yesterday that day of dread,
They took my friend, and now he's dead.
I tremble Lord, it's plain to see,
Today the victim will be me.

I hear their footsteps coming near,
O Lord my heart is full of fear.
I need you more than I can tell,
To free me from this earthy hell.
Great God who brought the world to birth,
And all the creatures of the earth.
Who made the stars, the moon, the sun,
Please let me die before they come.

'Prayer Of A Laboratory Animal' - acknowledgement to ANN SIMS

James Thompson

Noah's ark reminds us that God had more room in His structure of salvation for animals than for people. The Christian Churches, both Roman and Reformed, Catholic and Calvinist, have 'booted them out'!_

Church folk have NOT evolved from Noah's day. In fact, they've seriously regressed from the high aspirations of Old Testament prophets. Choosing the least noble of biblical passages, they've encouraged horribly barbaric practices: e.g., eating dead animals! Consequently, they've neither been healthy in a spiritual, mental nor bodily sense; and their diseases will worsen parallel with their increasingly sophisticated cruelty- until their conscience is awakened and they, at last, begin to reflect a dominion over the animals, expressive of the Good Shepherd's protective dominion over us!

Such is merely one of the many themes of this book-simply written for all, yet biblically supported for advanced Bible students. It is the humble and imperfect work of a leading Christian animal activist, frequently addressed on both TV and radio as "the animals' padre".

£4.50   ISBN O 9523022 0 9

GOD HONOURING WAYS TO - "*PREVENT CANCER*" - AND
End this cruelty

A CLERIC'S CONTEMPT OF ANIMAL BASED CANCER RESEARCH

Author. Rev James Thompson.

By way of introduction:

The writer wishes to make it clear from the start that he is very sympathetic to victims of the most dreaded of human diseases in whatever form it manifests its ugly head. He is also sympathetic to relatives and friends of the afflicted. As one who has spent almost half of his active ministry in hospital chaplaincy work, he is more moved in sympathy than most! He is, however, a realist who sees through the false, and equally knows that no lasting good will come from cruelty towards the helpless.

A Cleric's Contempt of Animal Based Cancer Research

Organised, High-pressure Begging:

One can hardly buy a drink at a bar, purchase something from a shop counter, or walk down a shopping thoroughfare without having a round of containers displayed or dangled before one's very eyes! I am referring to those Cancer Research collecting boxes, the contents of which are used – after colossal expenditure for salaries and overheads are deducted – to finance research which includes torturing helpless animals.

Can good come out of cold-blooded evil? Most folk would say Surely not!' Alas, the vast majority who donate to this number One charity con are ignorant of the fact that their kind donations are to further this abominable practice. They no doubt have in mind a precious loved one who died of this dreaded killer disease, as well as possibly the grim thought that they also might someday fall victim to it. Consequently, the sooner a cure is reached the better!

Not only is Cancer Research content with amassing fortunes by means already mentioned, but in most towns of even moderate size they have also established their own shops.

The very churches of our land, dedicated to the glory of God, are also repeatedly being used by these same registered 'charities' to further amass their fortunes. This is done by mourners repeatedly being encouraged to 'take up' in lieu of flowers for the deceased, a collection within God's house, NOT for the church which frequently struggles to keep its doors open, but for the objectives of these exceedingly affluent research foundations.

Advertisements within national newspapers of top circulation, are frequently displayed at tremendous expense – all to further influence the gullible public to hand over their money. 'Tear jerking' methods are frequently used, and if top publicity and advertising techniques are a means of swaying the gullible public to part with their hard-earned money then societies such as the above will use their expertise to the hilt.

One could write a great deal more, but enough has been mentioned to make the reader in no doubt whatsoever that the leading British cancer research societies mean business, and **are** in big business. Back in 1986 the Cancer Control Society affirmed:

'Large scale nationwide advertising is bringing into the four main established cancer charities in Britain something like £46 million a year. Together they hold assets of more than £76 million, including widespread international investments and building such as their various prestigious London headquarters'.

Yet, in the same year Dr Linus Pauling – two times a Nobel Prize winner – is quoted as affirming:

'Everyone should know that most cancer research is largely a fraud, and that the major cancer research organisations are derelict in their duties to the people who support them'

But, Haven't They A Right To Be Financed?

Yes, "the labourer is worthy of his hire". Such are the words of Scripture and the writer as a clergyman has no quarrel with that. However, when one considers the lucrative salaries of those employed in cancer research, and, (once massive overheads concerning the machinery has been deducted!) I refer to 'the vivisectors' themselves, then one has a right to feel deeply grieved. They could hardly be classified as 'labourers'!

Animal torturers (vivisectors) do not do their grisly work for a mere pittance. Indeed, their life style is higher than that of the average donor. What is more, they are frequently employed – year after year – daily torturing animals, with little more than a pretext that a possible 'cure is just around the corner'. And it would be fatal if the funds ran out before! It would also be the end of their careers if a cure was found!

In the USA, there are actually more people involved in the care, treatment or research of cancer than there are those with the disease itself, and we are little behind. The words of Dr Alec Forbes are most apt:

"The old idea that a doctor should 'first do no harm' has been forgotten, and it has been justly said that 'more people live off cancer than die of it'! It is no wonder that the public is beginning to revolt against such barbarous treatment"

No less an authority than Dr A Sabin – developer of the polio vaccine – writes:

'The cancer research bodies cause pain and suffering to hundreds of thousands of animals every year by inducing in the animals, by chemicals or radiation, large cancerous growths in their bodies and limbs. Giving cancer to laboratory animals has not and will not help us to understand the disease or to treat those persons suffering from it'

Gandhi unequivocally said. 'Vivisection is the blackest of all crimes'. Martin Luther King said, 'to condone evil is to be as guilty as to perpetrate it!

In giving money to cancer research You, dear reader, are not merely condoning evil but you are actually financing it to be perpetrated. Without money the vivisectors (they are no saints! – quite the opposite), would mostly cease doing their vile work. By donating to 'animal based' cancer research – although you've most probably never realised it before – You have been furthering the torture each day of God's helpless creation. However, what was done out of ignorance is surely pardonable!

A Future Day of Reckoning:

Let not the desire to appear generous, or to look magnanimous before others, lead you into donating as much as one penny more towards this diabolic work. Do not let timidity or fear of being cornered, make you feel it's the easiest way out just to give something small. In the name of the Compassionate, adamantly refuse to display such begging boxes. Consider the evil that you would be furthering, and that someday we will all be required to give an account for our deeds before the Good Shepherd Himself! For a day of reckoning will surely follow each one of us, as does the night the day!

The Bible clearly teaches, as does every Church, that God is a moral God; that "whatever a man sows that shall he reap", and that the quantity of the latter will far outdo the former. "Sow to the wind but reap the whirlwind", is the warning for men and nations contained in the divine volume. And the pages of history confirm it.

The God of the Bible is expressed through many analogies, but the chief of these is through the way far off herdsmen cared for and protected life considered inferior to their own. Yes, "The Lord is my shepherd"; that is the supreme analogy. And the Son of God applied it to Himself: "I am the Good Shepherd".

Yes, such far off herdsmen frequently risked their lives for the welfare of four legged creatures. What a divine commendation of their character! And with it, what an awful indictment surely falls on those who brutally exploit animal life today. And surely none more so than vivisectors! Yes, animals believe in God: of that the Scriptures are clear. As for the devil, for them he must surely be in the form of a vivisector!

Does The End Justify The Means?

Cancer researchers blatantly affirm that it is right and proper to amass funds to torture animals – as through so doing, humans may benefit. It's the old affirmation once attributed to the Jesuits: 'the end justifies the means'! But, I ask: IF the human family were to benefit 'physically' through such diabolic research, at what cost to its soul?

The Nazis who rationalised using helpless Jews as 'laboratory tools' so as to medically advance an assumed 'master race', lost far more in the process than they'd ever sought to gain. They stifled all sensitivity by viewing their victims as vermin; and the sluice gates of sadism were unlocked. They came near to gaining the whole world and they lost their own soul.

IF some minor forms of treatment have come about through animal torture and experimentation – though have no doubt about it, cancer is more prevalent today than ever before – then the crucial question is:

HOW MUCH FURTHER WOULD WE HAVE ADVANCED IF WE'D FOLLOWED AN HONOURABLE PATH OF RESEARCH: ONE PLEASING TO A MORAL GOD WHO CHOSE THE NAME OF 'GOOD SHEPHERD?'

Meanwhile, research still persists along a crooked, cruel path, and the following words of Dr Vernon Coleman are most apt:

Since Bernard Peyrilhe did the first cancer experiment in 1773 and injected a dog with cancer fluid from a breast cancer, thousands of researchers have tested new drugs and new techniques and have searched for new cures and new breakthroughs. There has certainly never been any lack of money for their efforts.

But what contribution have these researchers made to the battle against cancer? It is difficult to find any evidence that they have made any contribution at all. The number of people dying from cancer continues to rise annually. The number of different, known cancers also continues to increase.'

The Virtue of the Alternative Therapies:

Dr B.A. Richards affirms: 'Considered in the broadest terms, orthodox cancer treatment today is a failure and a disgrace. Contemporary cancer management in a number of respects, constitutes professional malpractice'.

Conventional therapies, which are the fruits of the vivisectors torture chamber, are known to us all. They are poisoning (chemotherapy), burning (radiation), and cutting (surgery). Yet, a recent survey taken of cancer therapists revealed that, put in the position of their patients, most of them would refuse their own treatment!

The most hopeful strides concerning a lasting cure appear to frequently come from complimentary therapies of the alternative approach. And yet these alternative therapies are usually only turned to as a last resource! With their bona fide Practitioners – including those as diverse as acupuncturists and aromatherapists and hypnotherapists – none of whom would, morally, stoop to torturing the defenceless of God's creation; need one wonder that the Good Shepherd's blessing rests on their labours!

Within the actual domain of cancer research, skin tissue and cell culture techniques – the equipment often encouraged and generously donated by animal welfare associations – has resulted in very large strides having been accomplished, and for this we can be extremely grateful. But, the world of what is known as alternative or complimentary medicine (touched on above), is making such tremendous strides that more and more young conventional GPs are being won over to incorporate several of its therapies. Such methods – until recently viewed as anathema – are being dispensed in place of drugs. This is much to the annoyance of the drug, chemical and vivisection empires. Incidentally, concerning the first, it is affirmed by

British-based Animal Aid that: 'There is one drug company representative for every eight GPs in this country; and every GP receives on average one hundredweight of advertising material per month.' I leave readers to draw their own conclusion!

Animal Testing Of Drugs:

The enlightened director of biostatics at Roswell Park memorial institute for cancer research in America affirms:

"Indeed, while conflicting animal results have often delayed and hampered advances in the war on cancer, they have never produced a single substantial advance either in prevention or in the treatment of human cancer."

The regius professor of medicine at Oxford University (Sir George Pickering) affirms:

"The idea, as I understand it, is that fundamental truths revealed in laboratory experimentation on lower animals are then applied to the problems of the sick patient. Having been, myself, trained as a physiologist, I feel in a way competent to assess such a claim. It is plain nonsense"

Yet, ignoring the wisdom of such men of eminence – and there are many more of like mind – within 1988 the Home Office statistics recorded no less than 259,648 animals having been used in cancer research in Britain.

God, as portrayed in Scripture, rewards the righteous and punishes the wicked. No lasting good will ever come from a mean deed, and if vivisection isn't a mean deed, what is! 'Though the mills of God grind slowly, yet they grind exceeding small!' (Longfellow) The side effects of drug therapy – the fruits of vivisection – are observable for all to see: Iatrogenic diseases cause a high percentage of admissions in any hospital, while dispensing of tranquiliser drugs, (assured to have been safe because tried out on animals) is resulting in tranquiliser addiction support groups having to be set up in nearly every prominent town and city. It would appear that the vengeance of a righteous God on behalf of the helpless of creation is becoming more evident.

'The wages of sin is death' say the Scriptures. The fruits of drugs such as Ativan, and the rest, are resulting in a living death! Yes, the Divine bill is coming well and truly home.

God Honouring Ways to Prevent Cancer:

Lung Cancer

To avoid one of our nation's second major killer diseases (heart disease rating first) the obvious factor for smokers is to immediately stop the vile habit.

Some have told the writer that they couldn't. However, once they were confirmed as victims of lung cancer, they had no difficulty. Regrettably, for them it was too late! If YOU are a smoker, stop now. A lady of seventy had smoked since fifteen; she came to the writer and after only two sessions in hypnotherapy has never smoked since! With some it may take longer.

If, for the sake of your pocket or purse, you consume synthetic products instead of the real food it seeks to imitate – via chemical colouring and flavourings, then you are putting wealth before health. It's an extremely silly thing to do. Make time to read the ingredients, and compare, before you purchase!

Smoked foods can cause stomach cancer. Pickled and highly spiced products are harmful. Natural fresh food is vastly preferable.

The fruit of past slave plantations has been handed down to us not only in tobacco but sugar. We use it in almost everything, and it simply says: God's food is imperfect, without man's condiments from the slave era added. Regrettably it is thrust on to us in as camouflaged a manner as is fat and offal from animal slaughterhouses. To avoid both is to be healthier.

Bleaching flour and rice to make them white results also in considerable impurity and loss of food value. White bread is NOT the staff of life but downright harmful.

Skin Cancer

Meanwhile, do not over indulge in sunbathing for vanity (be pleased with the colour God made you!). DO NOT USE animal-based soap, detergents or cosmetics – often the disguised offal of slaughterhouses to which are added chemicals, colouring and strong perfumes – or you are courting disaster.

Stress Induced Cancer

Should unconfessed guilt burden you then seek a reputable confessor or a well-balanced counsellor. Through past conditioning and false moral priorities, you could be bringing about inner punishment out of all proportion.

You wouldn't stop and make a meal on physical excreta in the street; you'd turn your mind from it as quickly as possible. Learn to react in the same way to those situations which are mentally akin to them. Your mind can only be churned up (creating havoc on the body) by what it chooses to focus on!

Whatever your employment or your daily pursuits, spend one day in seven – preferably when there is least noise and when dear ones can share it with you – to realise that you are on this earth for a purpose and not as a puppet to take up parking space. Determine to leave memorable and kind 'footprints in the sands of time'

At the end of each day count your many blessings. After all. You might have been born into a vivisectors cage! Pray for those poor creatures and seek God's guidance so as to make their lot a better one. True health and peace vibrates from the compassionate.

General Hints to Good Health

Be kind and caring to your body. You will never have another one in your life. One never fails to appreciate fully any part of it until that part goes wrong. If you are a Christian then you will recognise your body as the very temple of God Himself.

To assist with good health, affiliate to a sane place of worship; shop at whole food stores; avoid produce containing battery eggs, chemicals, white sugar and animal derivatives. Seek organic (certainly not pesticide 'protected' or chemically fertilised) fruit and vegetables. Buy only non-animal tested cosmetics. Such as those sold by 'Beauty Without Cruelty' and 'The Body Shop'. Cultivate positive thought patterns (via tapes, talks and visual imagery).

Too much alcohol can cause cancer. Tea and coffee (preferably decaffeinated) should certainly be in moderation, and they should never be drunk when very hot.

Try also to avoid radiation, chemicals and fumes. Take as much exercise in fresh air as possible. Vitamins A C and E are thought to be useful to help the immune system which suffers nowadays from all kinds of pollution.

These are simple yet important ways to bring about rejuvenation of body, mind and soul, and true health involves all three: 'wholeness of being'.

Preferring Darkness to Light:

The 'Good Book' refers to those who in later times will prefer darkness to light because their deeds are evil. Is not this applicable to those who either perpetuate or practice animal-based research into cancer? The utter hopelessness of such research has been stated previously. "Why is it then", you may surely ask, "that such archaic and barbaric methods are continued?" The following words quoted from a reputable naturopath Patrick Rattigan N.D. are surely well worth considering:

'Although cancer is preventable and has never been incurable by naturopathic means, vast fortunes are to be made by inducing artificial tumours in animals and by attacking the tumours with the cut/burn/poison package.

By deliberately looking in the wrong direction, the Cancer Business is maintained. The multitude of highly paid researchers, drug makers, salesmen, prescribers, surgeons, radiation machines manufacturers and operatives, animal breeders and equipment makers, aided by agents in government, health departments and the mass media, supress, or attempt to discredit all information on the rational, non-lethal approach to cancer.' (The Cancer Business)

Add to the above the animal-based cancer research charities who offer 'excellent' earnings to supervisors and others, and it all adds up!

Doctors Unite Against Vivisection:

Thankfully, in January this year (1990), at a time when some scientific doctors – **who are non-medical** – are still foolishly affirming that some vivisection is essential for progress, a new movement of protest amongst medical people: hospital doctors, GPs, vets, pharmacists – and other health professionals, has been established in the UK to oppose archaic barbarity. Their association is called: DBAE (Doctors in Britain against animal experiments).

The aims and objectives of such a movement happens to have much in common with an earlier movement which has made considerable progress in Germany, and other parts of the world, due to the dedication of an ex-resistance worker and friend of the writer – Christa Leipold of Frankfurt: 'Doctors Against Vivisection'

Yes, a younger generation of general practitioners and other doctors is coming round to an outlook scientifically akin to my own: that the metabolism, make up, life style and food of animals varies so much amongst their species, and is so very different from ours, that to artificially implant or create alien cancers within them, and from such effects seek to treat humans, is doomed to disaster from the start. Such logic and practices should be delegated to the Dark Ages where they started over 200 years ago.

Every Christian Must Act:

Friend, thank you for taking the time to read this booklet; may it move you to bitterly repudiate the aims of animal-based cancer research; and may you be led of God to warn others of this evil which the relevant charities are **still** using their funds to promote.

Let us fight on behalf of Him who as good shepherd embraces the whole of creation; whose ark provided refuge for far more beasts than mankind: whose covenants were within the former as well as with the latter; whose eye grieves over a fallen sparrow; whose angel appeared to a despise ass; whose son rode an untamed donkey through a hysterical crowd; and who, at the last, is figuratively referred to as a lamb!

With a Clear Conscience

You can help cancer victims via Cancer Relief, Anchor House 15-19 Britten St, London. And you can help modern cancer research by donating to ethical humane, non-animal research charities such as:

Dr Hadwen Trust for Humane Research
6C Brand Street
Hitchin
Herts

Humane Research Trust
Bramhall
Cheshire

Lord Dowding Fund for Humane Research
51 Harley St
London

For a comprehensive list of all the humane non animal research charities, send sae (plus a possible donation!) to a most worthy cause:

Disabled Against Animal Research & Exploitation
PO Box 8
Daventry
Northants NN11 4R

PRAYER FOR CANCER VICTIMS:

Eternal God, compassionate and caring, have mercy on those afflicted with this evil. Show us how best to help them. Save us from slanting them towards self-pity. Grant us the inspiration always to impart words of positive outlook whatever their situation. Teach us to know that the prayer of faith can still heal the sick; that what the mind accepts has a dramatic effect over the body. Teach us to know that we can always be positive in every situation for nothing is impossible with Thee. Give us the conviction of the psalmist: that it is better to trust the Lord than have confidence in man. And grant that on each of our visits we may know that we've taken You with us and left a closer consciousness of Your peace and presence with them.

O God, make your children aware that you are with them in the darkest of tunnels and in the loneliest of valleys, and teach us to put our hand into Yours for it upholds the whole universe. Amen.

PRAYER FOR LABORATORY ANIMALS

Gracious God whose analogy of self was in terms of how shepherds of old treated other species committed to their charge. Shame animal experimenters of their evil; move the hearts of Christians to rise up in rightful indignation; restore to your church the prophetic zeal that publicly rebukes cruelty while priests, wrapped up in rituals, condone it. By your arm destroy vivisection from our land, as you once did slavery and child labour. Thou whose Son didst liberate the animals about to be sacrificed in the Temple, bless and guide those who liberate animals from a far worse sacrifice today. Amen.

Other publications, By The Same Author, to awaken people to the evils practised throughout Christian Britain upon God's animal creation include:

RETREAT FROM RESPONSIBILITY (for spiritual retreatants to ponder) at 19p

THE BIBLE, THE CHURCH & THE ANIMAL KINGDOM (what the Bible teaches concerning animals, why the churches have actually encouraged their exploitation, and what to do to alter things) at £2.47

PRAISE FOR CREATURES GREAT & SMALL (much publicised pet lovers hymnal & devotional) at £2.28

A CLERIC'S CONTEMPT FOR CRUEL SPORTS (leaflet) at 75p for 10.

'Ty Coch'
Fron Park Road
Holywell
Clwyd
CH8 7UY

Reflections of a Spiritual Tramp

A compilation of passing thoughts from the unique life of
James Thompson, The Animals' Padre !

Reflections of a Spiritual Tramp

A compilation of passing thoughts from the unique life of

James Thompson: The Animals' Padre

Grateful thanks to my Wife and helpmeet Doreen for her typesetting; and also to the Delyn Press (Frontispiece is within Brynford Pet Cemetery, Holywell 01352-710500 'where pets are laid to rest in dignity')

Across the fields of yesterday he sometimes comes to me
A little lad just back from play, the lad I used to be.
And yet he smiles so wistfully, once he has crept within;
I wonder if he hopes to see the man I might have been?

Thomas S Jones

James Thompson ©1996
Ty Coch Publishing
Fron Park Road
Holywell
Clwyd CH8 7UY

Are My Footprints Clear and Noble?

Lives of great men all remind us we can make our lives sublime. And departing, leave behind us, footprints on the sands of time.

I well remember first coming across these words in a crisp new school book when I was at school in Coldstream and no more than eight years of age. Not only did factors such as the smell of a new book, the atmosphere of a classroom and the kindness of a teacher impress me then, they left indelible impressions for later years.

As a school leaver I longed to enter the printing trade, and I hear the swish of the treadle press still, just as if I were working for Arnold Williams at Holywell with dear Mr Blackwell composting nearby.

Indeed, I have sought to show love and care during several periods as a teacher and a lecturer. And, - over and above it all – the above quoted words of Longfellow have frequently slipped back into my mind like a ghost from the past, and I ask myself: "What footprints am I leaving in order to better the world that I'm so swiftly passing through?"

Almighty God has been exceptionally good to us and we must all, at the last appear before this Good Shepherd, to give account of our stewardship for our sojourn upon this planet. 'Is it a better place because we've lived upon it as human beings?' 'Will the animals and the birds weep at our departure?' Will little children have found it a safer, lovelier place because we've shared this world with them?' OR, on the contrary, have we plundered, indeed raped, much of the creation so that – like a business acquaintance – having built more business barns through ruthlessness and greed, one ends up spiritually destitute?

Have I, as a Christian, chosen a cushion in preference for a cross? Am I merely sitting back while parts of Britain become Europe's nuclear dumping ground? Is it true that I couldn't care a toss about our children's health and safety? While others vehemently protest about nuclear dumping, and are prepared to go to prison for the cause, am I –

in an influential position – simply burying my head in the sand? God forbid!

How CAN professing Christians sit back and clap hands for Jesus while the world for which he died is threatened with nuclear contamination? How far do I emulate the character of the one who called himself the Good Shepherd?

Are our lives no better than those Old Testament priests who gave a false veneer of religiosity to the decadence of their day? How far is my life's work and character synonymous with those prophets, apostles and martyrs?

God 'save us all' from becoming spiritual jelly fish – void of all straightness and backbone.

Working On All Cylinders!

Humans created in God's image are tripartite creatures. I mean they were designed to run on three cylinders and to view life in three dimensions.

Because of the lack of a spiritual dimension to life the masses appear to be existing on two cylinders. Sluggishness and jerkiness is the momentum of their journeying through this world. Indeed, they wear themselves out in the process and hinder other traffic desirous of passing them.

As the occupants of such a badly performing vehicle view the vista ahead, they find it as unattractive as did I: when having once screened, as an A.B.C. projectionist in Belfast, a colourful panoramic film, I had to follow it up with a flat picture in black and white: And, indeed, who wanted to listen to monotone after full stereophonic sound!

The masses in their saner moments occasionally sense that their lives are incomplete. They've, somehow, lost a quality they possessed at infancy. All that remains is a disorientated mind swayed by bodily appetites. And as nature abhors a vacuum, in this Aquarian age a non-Christian spiritual dimension becomes a real attraction

To those who are 'cheesed off' with a mental materialism that's left us spiritually bankrupt. Earth goddesses, pyramids and covens are, however, a poor substitute indeed for the spiritual life that the Good Shepherd came to impart.

Other folk are to be found, seeking to compensate for this lack of spiritual dimension, hooked on drugs, alcohol and promiscuity. However, seeking freedom they become horribly enslaved to their pet addiction, and they become almost oblivious to everything else around them.

St Augustine summed up such a situation most aptly: *'Though hast created us for Thyself O Lord, and our minds are restless until they find their rest in Thee'.*

Very sadly, the vast majority who run our councils, rule the country, teach the young and advise the married are (apart from occasions such as civic duties!) non worshippers. Yes, without that vital spiritual dimension they endeavour to run the economy, teach others, or be agony aunts. Consequently, their fruits are all around us!

The 'merry go round' which humanism and secular science have created, has evolved into a monster gone out of control. The perpetrators can no longer tame it; and providing they get their 'wage packet' – I think I could be forgiven for saying – they care little for the world, the environment, or the little children doomed to inherit it.

The Cliff Richards and Johnny Cashs of this world had all the prominence and high lifestyle that stardom could offer them, but they knew not the meaning of living on all cylinders; they saw not life in full dimension until they came to the greatest Star of all: Jesus of Nazareth. In choosing Him for their heyday they had, materially, everything to lose and nothing to gain. But having counted the cost, they accepted that Good Shepherd's spiritual life into their very hearts, and they've never looked back since. Dull religion would never have attracted such men of prominence, but winsome compassion of that humble Nazarene was a completely different matter!

Picking Out Gnats & Swallowing Camels

Prophets have, mistakenly, been viewed as little more than foretellers of the future. In actual fact, within the Old Testament, they were more concerned about the era in which they lived! The 'spirit filled' prophet was NOT one who worked himself into a frenzy, to possibly utter nonsensical gibberish. He was a champion for the oppressed and was able to read 'the signs of the times'.

Well, what do we read with a prophet's mantle today? I see a future ahead filled with possibilities for evil or good. I see a political world making incredibly quick changes, and people in cold war with each other holding on to nuclear creations which leak as they further corrode. I see a European community where helpless and defenceless forms of life, both human as well as animal, are exploited and horrendously mistreated. I see Christian circles alongside of these evils, more akin to euphoric drug covens, than being the salt of the earth and the mouthpiece of the helpless! Indeed, I wonder how long our heavenly Father will allow it to exist; and without seeking to frighten anyone, I perceive that we are all living over a nuclear time bomb – by the law of averages – overdue for going off!

However, optimistically from a New Testament viewpoint, I am able to look up because Christ may well return for His bride – the elect out of each denomination, and from none! So, if ever there were a need for people to get their priorities right and 'prepare the way for the Lord' it is surely now! And I realise there are many who feel they have done this already. Indeed, they have certainly 'made a covenant with Messiah by sacrifice'. They rejoice, so to speak, that they are 'sheltering under His blood' – nothing less than that of Calvary. However, the image of a first century's care is difficult to discern in their character! They are hardly preparing the way for His millennium Kingdom! They pray, 'Thy kingdom come' but as for a Paradise restored where the meek dwell without war and a lion eats straw as the ox, it's quite foreign to what they stand for. One group of believers anathematises another and vegetarianism is quickly dismissed!

Give it to them, there are evils which their brand of Christianity WILL denounce. There are the terrible sexual evils (admittedly, masturbation is losing its retributive results of blindness and insanity!) But we still have the utterances of four-letter words, the wearing of a Durex in over-populated countries, the non-attendance at mass on a day of obligation or the over indulgence in Alcoholic beverage. These things remain as Christian vice – but what about our commonest beverage – milk? Is the artificial insemination of cows every year a sin? No! Is the stealing of their calves at three days old to be shipped abroad for possible veal crating a sin? No!

Jesus denounced the religious leaders of His day because they went round 'picking out (immoral) midges while they chose to swallow (immoral) camels whole. We are no better!'

The Sanctity of Man's Beast of Scorn

While serving a curacy in Doncaster I often visited a wonderful gentleman of mature years – a retired miner who reiterated the story of a pony's refusal one morning, to enter a certain coal seam.

This seemed most unusual, and the miner beat the creature, only to be filled later with remorse on learning that a serious roof fall had occurred at that seam a few moments previous.

Perhaps the miner's experience was not unlike that of Balaam, whose ass refused to budge because an angel, unperceived by him, was perceived by his donkey!

Yes, an animal belittled as stupid by sinful men was chosen to witness the Nativity; and later, Jesus rode such a beast – which had never been mounted before – through a hysterical crowd and into the Holy City.

One of my most moving experiences was not on a pilgrimage to a shrine, but – believe it or not – to visit a little dog's grave: I have been to Greyfriar's Churchyard in Edinburgh to pray at the side of little Bobby's headstone; and I have considered how that little dog returned each night and day to its master's grave – and received the freedom of the city.

Call me a fool, if you will, but at the side of that grave I made a vow to speak up on behalf of dumb creatures and include them in my prayers and hymns.

Enlightened prophets of today (regrettably there are few around!) will refuse to limit God's salvation to their own species, just as their predecessors of old refused to limit it to their own race.

Unfortunately, the Church has refused to evolve spiritually. Priests will give a veneer of respectability to the corruptions of contemporary society by going through the motions, and I think I can still hear Jeremiah protesting – "And my people love to have it so!"

When fishes flew and forests walked
And figs grew upon thorn,
Some moment when the moon was blood,
Then surely I was born.
With monstrous head and sickening cry,
And ears like errant wings,
The devils walking parody
On all four-footed things.
The tattered outlaw of the earth
Of ancient crooked will.
Starve, scourge deride me: I am dumb,
I keep my secret still
Fools! For once I had my hour!
One far fierce hour and sweet.
There was a shout about my ears,
And palms before my feet.

G.K. Chesterton

Prayer in a Haunted Cinema!

The Prince of Wales was an eerie cinema, perhaps, because it contained some of the atmosphere of an old music hall. Preparing films on a Sunday evening, when no performance was allowed was certainly an eerie experience; but it saved a teenager coming into work on Monday mornings, and an extra lie in bed meant a lot! Consequently, I would frequently climb up the fire escape on the outside of the building in order to enter the re-wind room door.

Once inside, while making up the programme on the bench, I would become extra conscious of a dark passage behind me. It led into the projection room and, then beyond it, out into the old circle. One could repeatedly hear noises in the distance while making up the order of programme for the next day's performance; and humming was often a means of retaining sanity. But then, I dare say, an equally frightening experience occurred each week night when I was left in the old cinema by myself at the end of the evening's performance:

Most lights would be switched off before coming down from the back of the circle. Then, all other employees having left by the front entrance, it was my task as the youngest to bolt the swing doors after them. With the light of a torch, I would knock off the master switch and then grope my way into the large auditorium. It was then necessary to make one's way down towards the region of the massive red curtains surrounded by a gold engraved proscenium. When I reached side of the massive screen, I had to descend the side of the long disused orchestra pit. One went gingerly through a door and along a dusty passageway past dressing rooms, the contents of which were covered in cobwebs. They hadn't been used for years! But some doors that were ajar resulted in the light of my torch being reflected back from an old fashioned make up mirror in which I saw myself.

And, as if this were not enough! On reaching the end of that passage, one was confronted with an opening where stairs led up to the disused stage above, which contained ropes and old scenery: some containing masks.

Indeed, as a later employee once remarked: "You were always wise if you kept your eyes from looking up those stairs lest some ghost was to be seen standing at the top, gleaming down at you."

Noises on such occasions were often heard. You sought to interpret them as nothing worse than that of a stray rat or a contraction in the heating system. One dare not think otherwise. And strangely enough, though far from entertaining Christian belief, out of sheer desperation I found myself praying to God. This was not out of any sense of love or loyalty to Him. It was because I was frequently quaking in my shoes and could be no more an infidel than were far off soldiers at the battle front!

Indeed, I remember that a prayer of gratitude followed – after I'd nightly pushed open an old stage door; felt the peace of the cool night breeze; and focused on the balminess of what was frequently a star-spangled sky.

Churchianity's Shrivelled Deity!

The role of the Israelite prophet was vital, but often unpopular. The prophets denounced evils which went hand in hand with worship. Shrines were frequented, rituals performed and ceremonial went in full swing while the helpless were exploited and multitudes starved.

I feel that prophets like Amos, Elijah and Daniel are almost non-existent within today's Church; because multitudes in the world are living below the poverty line while affluent Christian civilisations spend billions to combat the ills of over indulgence.

Suffering is not confined to humanity – animals are brutally tortured to produce cheap food for man. Concrete animal 'Belsens' multiply, laboratory animals are blinded – and all this is often condoned by those who seek assurance that their sins are forgiven, and that a comfortable niche is reserved for them in Heaven.

The hypocrisy of Victorianism, which conciliated regular worship with child labour and industrial inhumanity, and the brutality of slavery with the daily reading of the family Bible, still manifests its ugly head, though in a more disguised and subtler form.

Christendom has become stinted. It has not evolved sufficiently. It has still to learn that God's love and care is no more exclusive to the human species than it was once thought to be to the Jewish race. Indeed, you can no more seek to confine the true God's influence and domain to a species or a race to a tabernacle, an altar or a chapel!

The whole of creation is God's concern. As the song-writer aptly expressed it: 'He's got the whole world in His hands'. And, consequently, when nailed to a cross, the Good Shepherd stretched out His lovely hands, figurative of the extent of His embrace and died for the whole world – not merely for a puny, pious 'self-styled elect of humanity!

A Christian's dominion over 'lower' forms of life, then, should be a reflection of Christ's dominion over us! Or of a Christian husband's dominion over the Woman he is called to cherish, protect, and possibly die for! It is, similarly, comparable to the dominion that Christian parents are expected to have over their offspring. Yes, it is all a dominion which is to be wed to a caring stewardship. An authority which protects and nourishes defenceless or weaker forms of life around.

Heaven help us if Christ's dominion over us were to be practised as we do our own dominion over the animals! Indeed, if that were to be the case, He would no longer be viewed as a good shepherd, but more appropriately, as a manifestation of the supreme adversary!

Conversely, I sense we can wholeheartedly agree with a previous Bishop of Manchester's sentiments, which he expressed within the House of Lords in 1975: - *"My Lords, I once heard it said – and the saying has haunted me ever since – that if animals believed in the devil, he would look remarkably like a human being".*

The Sanctity of the Simple Mind

Redemption is never dependent upon the ability to read and accept a scriptural formula of salvation or a denominational creed. It is knowing the Saviour of the Scriptures that matters as well as the Christ of the creed, and consciousness of the Good Shepherd's transforming presence is never limited by the inability to comprehend mental formulas.

It has been my experience, down through the years, to discover that the mentally retarded are frequently the spiritually most perceptive. Indeed, my son James was mentally damaged at an early age through medical negligence, incompetence, and the administration of too much oxygen.

When James was ten years old, on visiting a fairground, he could hardly wait to enjoy a go on the Noah's Ark! The ride was slower than usual as many children were aboard, but it was a trifle too fast for James's exceedingly unsteady feet. Consequently, he fell down upon the revolving platform as the hinged floor speedily moved up and down; and others of different ages either didn't notice what had happened, or what was more obvious – just didn't want to get involved!

But then, rushing across from the other side of the revolving merry-go-round, a fellow in his late teens or early twenties made a bee-line to the spot, by which time the ride was slowing down. The one who had come to our little lad's aid had lifted him up, caressed him, rubbed his poorly back; and was repeatedly asking him if he was OK!

Yes, James' rescuer was wearing, quite awkwardly, a ten-gallon type of seaside hat; and had soon replaced a straw back into his mouth! But one thing was obvious; a caring affinity was manifested from one retarded creature to another, at a depth seldom expressed between the professed normal.

On the other hand, to see the subnormal of this world frequently abused by the considered normal can be a harrowing and a soul-destroying experience. Indeed, I'm still haunted by the memory by a group of 'normal?' children on a campsite dancing round young James who was on a hillock. They jeered, taunted, and pulled faces, while in bewilderment, quietness and a heavenly innocence James looked so puzzled. And then – left alone – he began to smack his own hand as if he were to blame! Then, with a bewildered look, my little lad began to retract into himself. He began to realise that – for some unknown reason – he just wasn't made the same as other children.

I looked around and beheld my previous wife who'd followed me out of our tent. Her eyes were full and her features were extremely drawn. She said nothing, but one thing was obvious – she'd entered Gethsemane with Jesus!

In the world's eyes, James is sub-normally retarded. In the last century, when all but the ungodly attended church, the 'devout' would have put him far out of sight. But in James I truly see a deep innocence personified, a countenance that tells of a Divine presence closer than hands or feet.

Distorted Moral Priorities

If only people would read the Bible as it is, rather than through the vista of Latin fathers or Puritan reformers! We are still making the Word of God of none effect by the traditions of men.

Yes, and I sense we are still, from a moral point of view, 'picking out gnats while we swallow camels'. We engineer a whole host of discussion over liturgies and ministries while we swallow, hook, line, and sinker, man's exploitation of God's creation.

We fail to realise that what we sow as a race and species, we will undoubtedly reap. We have failed utterly to learn that life is basically sacred and interdependent, that to harm a part is ultimately to harm the whole.

God gave us human life and expects us to use it as faithful stewards within the world for which He gave His Son. Yet we exploit and abuse the larger part of creation using might as power.

We cram hens into cages where they are distorted into egg producing robots. We might even feed them with pellets containing their own excreta, if not the remains of their fellow creatures; and then we wonder why salmonella breaks out, why fresh killer diseases are on the increase. We might even have the audacity to question the justice of God in allowing us to suffer such retribution.

We perpetuate the horrific practice of vivisection and, paradoxically, expect physical health to come from moral sickness, good to be the reward for evil.

Christendom's prayers are confined to human need, and as for the animals which God cared for in his Ark and made two covenants, the churches have been unanimous in booting them out. Yet the prime analogy He gave of Himself so that others might recognise Him, is in terms of the ways a righteous man cares for the helpless of another species entrusted to his care.

Thankfully, a change is slowly coming. A newer generation which no longer interprets 'immorality' solely in sexual terms but with far more relevant priorities is rising; yes, to blacken today's hypocrisy as we blacken yesterday's which piously read its family Bible, worshipped, condemned the illegitimate, concealed the imbecile, covered each female leg and condoned children being sent up chimneys and down mines.

From similar blatant hypocrisy may the Good Shepherd deliver us!

A Cavern or a Cathedral!

Yorkshire's West Riding is a delightful area full of mystery with its beautiful landscapes, its hills, valleys and old mills. And as to be expected, it has its fair share of long tunnels. Who could have built a railway in such an area without having tunnelled through hills to come out into further luscious valleys!

One such tunnel at Marsden holds nostalgic memories for me. It's a reminder of years past when, as a young family, we occasionally travelled through it between Yorkshire and Lancashire, or walked nearby its alluring entrance at the side of the still canal.

Indeed, it could be quite an experience while taking the train journey, to be plunged into a long period of darkness; but the light and beauty which one witnessed on 're-surfacing' could be a glorious sight to behold.

That particular tunnel was a great feat in workmanship because the navvies who had built such a lengthy expanse through the Pennines were only equipped with the tools and implements of a bygone era. Indeed, many of them would never live to see the completion of their work. Most were of Irish stock, desperate to find employment of any kind. Yet such rough and ungainly navvies were not without a Faith which meant so much to them.

The years taken tunnelling through the rock seemed never ending, and as for coming out into the light at the end of each working day, the leisure hours were few and the distance was often too far to traverse to witness the light. However, they were hardy men for though they were enveloped by darkness they made the most of their situation.

A spacious cavern was created far within one of those tunnels; there was a parallel canal as well as two separate train tracks to consider; and the vast vault became not only a place to rest and sleep; it also became a rallying point for the celebration of their Mass. Consequently, for brief periods they transformed that cavern of darkness into a veritable cathedral for worship. From it they received spiritual illumination and sustenance with which to labour on.

Reader, if You are compelled to work for any period of time within a dark or uncongenial atmosphere, just think of those poor creatures with a lamp or candle in the nib of their cap and rock dust on their lungs; the trickle of water round their feet and a dampness and clamminess round their body which had their clothes sticking to them.

No doubt the thoughts of these abused creatures would often be of Ireland: of relations, wives and children whom they would possibly never see again. Yet, they used a vast cavern as a temple to God and they would realise, with simple child-like faith, that they were not alone. Yes indeed, a great spiritual light must have surely emanated on Sundays and holy days from that cavern within the deep bowels of darkness.

One couldn't help but feel a lump in one's throat as one considered those far off workmen; and all so that busy trains could rattle as trans-pennines escorting people, cattle and goods from one famous county to another.

Then how dare you or I moan about our petty setbacks when we compare our lot in life with what was theirs? I say: *How dare we!*

Much Evil Comes from Church Dogma!

Behaviour is very much influenced by belief. That is why crime goes up as deterrents decrease! Indeed, if all believed in the biblical doctrine of retribution as well as reward after this life, then behaviour in the present would greatly improve.

Where other faiths teach the possibility of returning in the form of another species, those species are given a respect denied to them within Christendom. Indeed, Christian theologians, many of whom have been influenced by Aristotle, will tell the faithful that factors which would trouble a Buddhist need not trouble us.

Much religious brain washing within formative years results in sexual malfunctioning and guilt. The guilt experienced, and frequently ignored at the conscious level, will not be ignored by the subconscious. The result – thanks to past religious leaders! – is that not only the practice of contraception – but simply its advocacy as a temporary solution for the Third World, may result in anxiety neurosis.

No such neurosis, however, would be felt by a vivisector through torturing animals, because even the most up to date Catholic catechism will assure him that no sin has been committed. The same branch of Christendom has consistently affirmed that animals neither have rights, nor a soul. As for the sounds of animals agonising in research laboratories, they can always have their voice boxes removed – as is the permitted case in church-going America!

If we allowed the Bible to interpret itself to us directly then we would find that the possibility of reincarnation is quite a real one: Jesus spoke of

Elijah having returned as John the Baptist: and he never rebuked the disciples for believing in a man being born blind because of a possible sin in a previous life (the teaching of reincarnation was not opposed until 553AD. This was at the council of Constantinople, and only by a very narrow majority).

So, all I am saying is that if we were as broad and tolerant in teaching as the Good Shepherd Himself, then bigotry and dogmatism would ease and the whole of creation would benefit. We would cease being parasites and be well on our way to partly restoring Paradise, in preparation for Messiah's return to come and rule.

Room For Nothing but Love

Rejection; yes, that was what the Holy Family experienced. There was no room for the birth of the Christ child in the village inn; thank God there WAS room for Him in the stable. For there amongst humble beasts of burden the Saviour of the world was born. While those chosen to witness the miracle were animals, and with them animal defenders: shepherds!

The Christ child was brought up to feel and witness an all-embracing love and care. His was NOT the lot to acquire the conditioned education of the day. It was first hand: witnessing the world of nature around Him; and that of human nature within His earthly father's workshop! As a consequence, Jesus became a shrewd observer of the natural world; and being nurtured in love from the beginning, the greatest true lover that this world has ever witnessed.

Jesus' home was the humblest and yet the most beautiful. He had a mother who loved Him all the way to the cross even though she couldn't always understand His motives. I dare say that Joseph did his best to provide his eldest with a homemade toy or two; but they had other children with mouths to feed. There was no security whatsoever. Yet, miracle of miracles, that home was the greatest of all, and I'll tell you why:

It was NOT a dormitory where the family lived separate lives during most of the day, only to see their offspring at night. Although the family became large the mother was far removed from that of modern baby producers: those who cultivate offspring battery style, with little cost to them but to everyone else! Yes, Jesus had a marked advantage over the 'little mites' born into today's world by self-motivated women who give priority to career, or pin money, before their child's most impressionable yet fleeting years.

Rejection of time and love so as to acquire money for gadgets, holidays and computer types of toys results in a new generation becoming computerised in character and style, with no more feeling or compassion than a talking dalek. God have pity on us; the very Soul of our offspring is being swiftly eroded.

It is only in turning to the example of Mary that civilisation can be saved from creating a generation of heartless zombies. A sadder and even more pathetic type than those who parade the streets today, so bored that they do damage; whose state education may have bloated their heads into baseballs but starved their characters into peanuts – a lethal combination!

Alas, they also are not to blame! The rot had already started when THEIR basic need of 'mother love' was largely denied. The diabolic advent of a communal surrogate-motherhood had just begun!

May each young mother learn to emulate the greatest of mothers. The ever-blessed Mother of Our Lord!

Does Church Reflect Her Shepherd?

As I awaken this morning and behold the snow outside, I become aware of the plight of the birds in seeking food for their young. In the distance I see a dog romping in the snow; and when I look down and see a spider scuttling along the bathroom floor, I simply realise how fortunate I am! Why the Gracious Almighty should have chosen to make me a human I just don't know! I only know, to quote His own Son's words. That 'To whom much is given, from him much will be required'.

What are we doing, for the benefit of creation, with our God given human talents? How embracing and compassionate is our Faith? Are we the mouthpiece for the dumb? Are we seeking to restore Paradise through paving the way for (what some might term) a Millenium? Or, do we plug our ears to Creation's groans solely to sing, to our own evangelical circle, choruses about a salvation procured at Calvary, and arrogantly interpreted as exclusive to ourselves?

> We are God's chosen few
> All others will be damned
> There is no room in heaven for you
> We can't have heaven crammed

In this era of renewed Bible interest, how much of our religion is akin to the prophet's dream, and how much has been horribly distorted through the theologian's lens? Perhaps we prefer a whole host of fallible Bible aids (as hopelessly abstract and spiritualised as Madam Baker Eddy's!) (founder of Christian Science) to that of a volume in which prose and poetry can, usually, be quite easily deciphered.

I wonder: do we prefer the H2O formula of the divinity hall to the crystal-clear water of life? Or is it some esoteric, mystical allegorism of a New Age guru to the clarity of Jesus' example and teaching as substantiated by four complementary writers?

Indeed, is the Holy Spirit capable of applying and interpreting the basic evangelical message to our individual hearts, or must He be confined to working along historically polluted channels? One thing is for sure: when Messiah returns, it is not only to take His faithful bride in white to the marriage supper, but it is also to denounce and pass judgement on the counterfeit. I refer to that vast religious accumulation which has usurped the character of Christ's bride. She is the one who has historically deceived the nations and is appropriately attired as a harlot in purple and scarlet robes!

The Bridegroom for which the Church prepares herself is none other than the Good Shepherd Himself. What He loves, she loves. His concern is hers. Their interests are identical. They are made for each other! Is YOUR church of like mind, compassion and outlook with the Christ who chose a stable for residence; whose birth was heralded by angels to animal protectors in the dark? If not, it may well be that you have been deviously brain washed under the harsh tyranny and cruel domain of a usurper.

Jesus said, "Every tree shall be known by its fruit." Has your church the kind of compassion that good eastern shepherds had in, far off, first century Palestine? If it hasn't. If it looks upon an animal straying into a church as a source of defilement and profanity, then you would do well to educate it along true Christian lines – always backing up your beliefs with scriptural support (I'm always prepared to help you!). And if this approach proves unacceptable, I strongly suggest you consider worshipping elsewhere.

Concern Starts at Coldstream

I wonder how YOU first got concerned with animal care? For myself, it was an accumulation of factors so that eventually the scales were tipped for action. Yes, it is so easy to talk and philosophise. There IS a place for such mental contemplation. However, unless our dreams are turned into deeds, we'll simply have generated emotional thrust merely to dissipate it. As harmful to our character and psyche as revving up a car engine without engaging the gear! 'DO great deeds, don't just dream them', was the advice of my genteel MUM when I was a junior; and I realise their importance fifty years later!

Sentiment towards animal suffering is more than futile unless it leads to action. It's no better than the Victorians who loved to 'weep buckets' over a melodrama in the music hall – but then, on their way home, they'd pass the street urchins without giving them a second glance.

My first thought concerning animals was when, around seven or eight years of age and living in the lodge of a beautiful private estate, I was out playing with our delightful wire-haired fox terrier. True to her instinct our pet, whom I'd taken for a walk by myself, came pounding back to me with a baby rabbit she'd caught squealing from beneath her teeth. And then, to my horror, I looked across the grass to spy mummy rabbit watching on with much emotion from outside her burrow. A spiritual battle appeared to be raging within the mind of Pat (that was our pet's name!). Then, looking up to me, she – with a sense of deep reluctance – allowed me to open her mouth and give up the creature which scuttled away, apparently none the worse for its ordeal; mummy and baby rabbit were reunited and hopped off happily together!

Indeed, it seemed as if the environment then changed into a wonderful glow and that nature had become vibrant with song. I sense I danced my way home accompanied by Pat; our pet whom I loved now even more than before. And when I narrated to Mum what had happened her eyes sparkled with pride, just like they did whenever I brought her wild violets, daises or even dandelions!

I thank God that I had a wonderful Mum. Though separated from a dad whom I hadn't as yet met, she endeavoured to fulfil a father's role as well as a mother's. At least she instilled into my pliable mind her concept of a true manliness. While sat on her knee, she would even sing:

> *So you want to know my laddie, what I would have you be,*
> *When the whole wide world's your playground,*
> *And you're big and strong like me:*
> *'To fight and face life's battles; win them if you can.*
> *But, first of all my laddie: 'be a man, be a man!'*

Alas, her concept of manliness was far removed from that to be confronted in my seafaring dad! Nevertheless, such was my first encounter with a situation that endeared me to the animal kingdom as well as further to herself. God forbid that anyone should underestimate that noblest vocation of motherhood! While frequent males taught that manliness meant insensitivity and hardness, Mum taught us that it meant protecting all creatures great and small, and particularly the defenceless, the crippled and the weak.

For What are we Prominent?

The ego within us to excel can be very strong. It can be used to bless others or to blight them.

In 1978 I encountered two kinds of prominence within two months. They concerned that gruelling experience of a job interview. The first was to acquire a post as a prison chaplain; the second, that of being invited to Number Ten for probability of a crown appointment.

The first interview resulted in being confronted by some prominent officials including the, then, home secretary who was in the vicinity. I was ushered along the front of a drab room, head level with a raised platform. Sharp questions were directed down to me; my head peered up to reply

Well, it was obvious that the answers I gave didn't impress some of the panel. I wished, as a potential prison chaplain, to assure them that though I had deep compassion towards penitent criminals I must never be mistaken for a mushy do-gooder! Indeed, I even elaborated on how I favoured corporal punishment for 'hard-liners'! "We need more of the glasshouse treatment" I said. Yes, as you can imagine, I was giving all the answers they DIDN'T wish to hear. So as the interview proceeded some sarcasm became less veiled, and I felt humiliated.

The questions having ceased I was then informed that a cup of coffee was available for me. However, I'd need change to operate the machine. It was along the outside corridor, but regrettably, I would not be able to return to it, to sit in the present room reserved for interview.

Well, I didn't avail myself of their 'generosity'. What was more, I was glad to breathe again the aroma of the London streets outside.

Within eight weeks and I was summoned once more to London. This time it was nowhere less than to Downing Street. I must admit that when asked by a Cockney, within a Tube train, as to where I was going, my stature grew in size as I turned and said "actually it's Number Ten!" Then, on reaching the 'hallowed' spot, tourists waving across to me, I waved back as if to bless them before being ushered in! Now I must admit, I wasn't being at all humble. But, in all honesty, clerical representatives of the Galilean are hardly guilty of hiding their light under a bushel!

Soon, I was led upstairs where a gentle though timid soul approached me, helped to take off my overcoat and then returned to ask whether I preferred tea or coffee. Well, I must admit 'it made my day'. When Mr Peterson (that was his name) then asked of I'd object to him asking me personal questions concerning my churchmanship, family life, etc. I felt more honoured than ever. And then, when he asked 'rather jovially' if he could fulfil the role of mother, pouring out the coffee and offering sandwiches and biscuits, I didn't know whether to laugh or cry.

On leaving Number Ten my host uttered words to this effect: "Whenever in London feel free to call round. Just ring in first so that these gentlemen on the door will know you are due to arrive". Alas, within twelve months and that wonderful gentleman had retired!

The point I make is simple this: within two months I'd come across two types of prominence. One was used to blight me and the other to bless me. If WE hold a position of prominence in the community, may it be channelled to bless others and not to blight them. May we manifest the power that possessed Christ; not that which possessed Herod!

Clergy and Their Turkey!

I well remember how, in my first country living, a brace of pheasants was once sent round to the Rectory from the, then, young Lord Scarborough. I offered a short and silent prayer for guidance; and then handed back the birds to his gamekeeper – along with appropriate words to convey! I wasn't at that stage a vegetarian but my opposition to any calculated form of animal cruelty had been well aired, and I had no intention to hobnob or possibly ease the conscience of those whose lifestyles clashed so openly with my own.

Indeed, I chose to dismiss as rector's warden (after twenty-one years) a gentleman farmer 'fond of the shoot'. I objected adamantly to him attending Matins complete with rifle. And in his place I put a humble, compassionate farm labourer: a manual worker, as was our blessed Lord.

I can assure you it didn't go down at all well. A most affected archdeacon was constantly at my door as well as down 'the blower'!

Today, in an age when few are unaware of the cruelty involved in Broiler house Belsens, and factory farm sweat shops, many clergy set an appalling example.

Indeed, leading clerics who sit down to a traditional flesh-eating Christmas dinner are perpetrating an appalling example to the nation. And, as if to add insult to injury, they reveal the heights of hypocrisy in offering grace over the same.

The loftier their position the graver must surely be their guilt! Yet one can hardly imagine a prelate of any episcopal province choosing a plate of nut roast for his Christmas dinner. They just don't appear to tally (though

Wales might delight us still!)

As for 'the deadly lusts of the flesh', they are not exclusive to sex, but involve the palate no less than the penis! A factor which those professing the 'superiority' of a celibate life frequently chose to ignore. Indeed, to have an innocent life slain for the sole gratification of one solitary meal – when wholesome alternatives are in wholesale abundance – is surely a most cruel and despicable thing to do!

The fact is, though, we've been horribly conditioned over the years to see no harm in it. In fact, up to two decades ago without meat on the plate I considered my dinner was void of essential nutrients; and all the doctors around – excluding castigated 'quacks'! – were only too keen to further this fallacy.

Church leaders have frequently been keen to tell 'the likes of myself' that one must never put the needs of mere animals before that of exalted humans. There seems to be a great pride in affirming this. However, such an argument – when relating to carnivore – is nonsensical. As it takes, on average, ten pounds of grain to convert into one pound of meat, surely they should be the first to propagate a vegetarian lifestyle, so as to speedily stop the starvation of humanity's millions.

In the light of the above, plus the scares of salmonella poisoning – and now the far more serious scourge of BSE! – to further, by example or word, any other than a vegan orientated vegetarian lifestyle, must be sheer irresponsibility.

Christian Care is More Than Human

I was in Germany two years ago, where I stayed with a delightful couple wrapped up with animal rightist activities. We attended a massive rally comprised of Christians from all denominations. "Dogmas and creeds have kept us apart for years" I preached, "but today's dogs and cats have brought us together!"

"Yes" replied another, "and if the churches this century had expressed the kind of compassion that's been expressed here today, two dreadful world wars between our countries would not have happened!" My mind went back to the memorable words of Albert Schweitzer: *'Until he extends the circle of his compassion to all living things, man himself will never experience peace'*

The world has been ravaged because of too much religious bigotry and too little Christian compassion. In Germany I experienced true spirituality while guest to this young couple who appeared over protective of a dog which was not, at first, the most charming of characters!

When I first approached this large hound, he snarled and portrayed a great set of teeth. "Yes, animals as well as humans need to be redeemed" I said to myself: "and I doubt whether you would have been included in the ark! – I'll pray for you!" Then, I later learned why the hound had every reason to be hostile to human strangers. He'd been horrifically mistreated by one in the past!

However, regardless of this dog's past, he was now being more pampered by his present mistress; and I have little patience with those who appear to go 'over the top' with one species to the exclusion of all others, humans included.

"I hope you don't mind", said Manwaila (our hostess), "but though you are exceedingly welcome to stay here for the whole week, I must slip out most nights until the morning!"

'What strange kind of work does our guest do? I later asked my Wife 'that our hostess should be missing five hours a night while working as a psychologist during the day!'

Before the week was over our curiosity had been solved. On a voluntary basis Manwaila was caring for prostitutes in a Frankfurt 'drop in', counselling drug addicts and even washing and dressing those afflicted with AIDS.

Yes, I should not have been surprised. For as Emmanuel Kant inferred: *'you can always judge the heart of another by that person's treatment of an animal'*. Jesus chose for Himself the title of an animal carer: a Good Shepherd; and when He died for the sins of the world, it undoubtedly included those of the animal kingdom as well. 'He has the whole world in His hand'.

I still love Anna Sewell's book: BLACK BEAUTY! It's the kind of literature children should be encouraged to read today for a better tomorrow! Words uttered by her are most apt: *'There is no religion without love, and people may talk as much as they like about their religion, but it does not teach them to be good and kind to animals as well as humans, it is all a sham'.*

God has made several covenant promises with the animals. 'Lord, save us from any profession of the Christian Faith which would ever seek to exclude them!'

Costly Discipleship!

The beginning of the year is frequently a time for making resolutions; and, indeed, what better a resolution than to put Christ first and foremost in one's life! Such a thought was uppermost in my mind when, as a mere youth, I decided to bring in the New Year within church. If others were to 'see out the old and bring in the new' within a public house, ought not the Christian to make his way to God's house!

Indeed, as I made my way on that cold slippery night down a very steep cobbled hill to where the parish church of St James stood, I felt a sense of sadness and pity for the bleary-eyed folk I passed who would, no doubt, have thought that an eighteen year old going to worship at such an unearthly hour must have been 'off his rocker'.

Well, I wanted God to know that I loved Him and that I was not only grateful for the past but more than grateful for all the future that awaited a young man. As I approached the church and heard the solitary bell ring I repeatedly said in silence: 'Lord thank you for the gift of life and for my awareness of You'.

Alas! On entering the building, the congregation was, I well remember, no more than fifteen in number (and that was in 1948!). The altar looked quite misty in the distance and when the hymn 'O God our help in ages past' was sung I was conscious of little more than its two flickering candles, plus the saintliness of Mr Daniel the curate who, with the vicar, led that worship. We later knelt and sang in contemplation; 'Lead us heavenly father lead us'.

Then, as we made our way out into the cool, crisp morning, it seemed as if bells from a belfry rang in unison.

Much later that morning – while preparing the films for the evening show within the local cinema – the members of staff, who knew me well, asked how many pubs I'd circulated the night previous. "You may think it strange", I inferred, "but I went to church instead!" I'd no doubt anticipated a pleasant sense of surprise. Instead, a deadly silence followed. I found myself literally deserted. The very last thing I'd wanted to do was to offend them, and they could never ever have termed me a 'holy Joe'.

I can only say that the more such a confession had brought a wedge between my work mates and myself, the more it was compensated for. Christ came very close, as if to say: 'You've done that for me. I understand your situation perfectly and I love you the more because of it'. In my own way – fighting back tears of gratitude – I would respond in this fashion: 'Lord Jesus I love you too; help me to always put you first in my life – regardless of the cost.'

I haven't been true to this wonderful God. Considering the light I have received, I've failed Him more than have most. However, 48 years later! – I intend to start another new year within His house. And, who knows, I might be as blest this time as I was then.

If there is to be a watch-night service in your church then perhaps you'd like to do similar. Do go along! There may be few present; there might be many! But Jesus will be there to meet You. If you're really in earnest, then you'll find Him as close and as real there as I found Him, those many years ago within lovely Holywell.

Mar Lodge Chapel, Braemar

The tour up Royal Deeside had been most entertaining. Our host, the bishop of the diocese had shown us round the pleasant rectory at Ballater. Was it to our satisfaction Would Doreen, as possible lady of the house, feel comfortable in it? Was the present décor to her taste, as funds were sparse!!

Well, time was passing; many miles had been traversed; and the joint church councils were eagerly waiting to meet us in a local hotel.

The Bishop, a well-loved man, cordially introduced us to a host of congenial people. One honourable lady eagerly advised me to spend some time with another dear soul whose late husband had held a high masonic post. One or two cultured gentlemen introduced themselves. Paté and chicken sandwiches were graciously handed round, minus all crusts, and during the chitchat I was asked more than once if I'd visited the 'delightful little chapel', so small and cute, known as St Ninian's! Indeed, I had; and its memory sticks vividly in mind.

Within the earlier itinerary of that same day the bishop had taken my Wife and I up a hill past many trees, where 'lo and behold', a herd of timid deer had majestically gathered. Then, as we came round a further bend of this secluded track a large Victorian style of mansion loomed up before us. "This is Mar Lodge" said the Bishop. "It is a hunting lodge and has within the grounds its own chapel. You would be expected to officiate here once a month"!

I there and then told him of my animal concern, to which he was sympathetic and in agreement. "However, this is part of their life" he affirmed. "They've known no other. Antagonism would be counter-productive. It would do no good. In fact it would alienate them!"

Soon, we entered the unique chapel. It was dark and small. My Wife and I looked towards each other as the head of deer and antler 'adorned' the house of God – along with heraldry and memorabilia of those whose blood lust required the breeding of so many, gracious, red deer.

Then, as our host directed us to the altar, he mentioned how a previous incumbent reminded him of myself. The fellow had been deeply loved as the Dean of the Diocese. So sensitive and caring was he to those who frequented Mar lodge, interjected an affable lady who'd joined us, that "knowing it was the birthday of a boy in the congregation, he got the worshippers to sing 'happy birthday to you'". This was then followed by communion; to be later followed by a hunt!

Well, I swore silently to myself that if given the post, I'd diplomatically (not my best quality!) seek an ally in Princess Diana who'd recently opposed her husband concerning blood sports. However, such was not to be! The post went to the other candidate whose affinities and interests made him more appropriate for the post. As for myself, I moved from Dewsbury to 'Granite City' where, as well as being Diocesan hospital chaplain, I would again swing incense, ring bells and give benediction: as parish priest of another industrial suburb. Great work; but alas, for my dear and wonderful helpmeet Doreen, a clergy house and district as far removed from Royal Deeside as the moon from cheese!

A Sign of Assurance near a Canal

I often think of my nine years as Vicar of Milnsbridge, a suburb of Huddersfield. It was a hard industrial parish, but it taught me a great deal within a short period of time. Opposition to my stand against animal cruelty had resulted in me leaving possibly the most affluent and picturesque parish within the Diocese of Sheffield. It appeared as if I'd stirred up 'a hornet's nest' led by the local, *so-called* Gentleman farmer and his buddy the Vet.

Well, taking on this new incumbency had incorporated also – as some form of compensation for its drabness – the chaplaincy of a delightfully new hospital. But **was** this poverty stricken and run-down parish a suitable base? One would hardly think so with redundant mills, and church buildings rotting and 'in the red'! Perhaps I'd been too rash in accepting it!

Although, like an Old Testament prophet I'd 'wrestled in prayer' before acceptance, I was already wondering if my heart had run away with my head! Within the first few weeks, I began to have further doubts on having moved from rural affluence to urban poverty. Well, perhaps God would give me some sort of sign; some mark of assurance that my life was definitely in the centre of His will! Well, it came quicker than I'd anticipated. In fact, it occurred later in the same week of mounting despair.

Arrayed in cape and cassock on a dull, damp morning; having visited the shopping region which was low down and interspersed with dark mills, I made the journey homeward, which included a steep street. In fact I was nearing the start of it, having just crossed an old canal bridge when something memorable occurred: a bright little fellow approached me.

Though so small and young, this little fellow's eyes were all 'a goggle'. They actually sparkled as he came over to me. In fact, it would appear as if he'd just seen a vision. Then coming up to my side he gently touched my cassock. "Yes it is; isn't it? I know you. Don't I? I know who YOU are" he said. And then, with eyes of ecstasy he looked up into the sky. He raised his finger upwards and glanced briefly to the heavens: "**You've** come from up there!", he said.

Well, I smiled and said nothing. I was stunned and would not have wanted to dash such joy from that innocent face. So he made his way round me to further his journey; and as he looked back he appeared as a little angel in poor clad clothes.

Well, as for myself, I wanted to cry; I felt so humble. But I now knew that God HAD given me a sign of assurance. I WAS in the centre of His will. I WAS in the parish where He wanted me. The little fellow had considered me to be Jesus. What a standard to live up to! And how impossible with soul destroying, backbiting, power seeking church council meetings which later follow! But they are another story. Sufficient to say: I've seen the very devil in them. But that day, near the canal, I saw Christ in that little urchin on the cobbled street. I wonder where that precious soul is today!

What We Are, And What We Say

"What you are speaks so loud I can't hear what you say!" These words uttered to a professing Christian express a warning to those of us who seek to win others for our Lord and Master.

There are two ways of witnessing. The first is propositional and the second is relational. Those who advocate the first are frequently keen to forcefully express a biblical formula; the acceptance or rejection of which determines one's destiny – not for time, say some, but for eternity! Such enthusiasts often have the push of high-pressure reps, witnessing by a cheesy smile reminiscent of an advert for toothpaste. They have their place and, give them their due, Christ is 'verbally' proclaimed. Of that there can be no doubt.

For myself, I prefer those who preach Christ primarily without words. It might sound heretical but I only know that those who made Jesus real to me did so because I wanted and received the spirituality they unmistakably radiated and conveyed. Indeed, for those unable to appropriate doctrine or creed – and that includes all the mentally incapable, the non-evangelised and the animals too – Jesus becomes real when preached non verbally.

However, I do not expect us to become mute believers! Verbal expression of our Faith has its rightful follow up. I simply suggest that we preach primarily by our presence and pursuits. And then, when eagerly asked by others why we so tick, that we follow it up by scriptural support or creedal affirmation.

A fellow I deeply admire, from the annals of modern history, was a shy, quietly spoken little man – plagued with ailing health plus curvature of the spine. The forceful, outspoken Dr Johnson once contemptuously referred to him in Parliament as "that whimp of a man". Time, however, confirmed that William Wilberforce was a spiritual giant. As for his loud critic, he would be unworthy to stand as a spiritual pygmy at his side.

The churches have had their loud and verbal Aquinas's, Loyola's. Calvin's and Knox's. Would that they might have had more of the quieter and more radiant St Francis's, Gladys Aylward's, Albert Schweitzer's and Mother Theresa's!

Some believers recently called Ian Paisley, Ulster's John the Baptist! Well, I remember a Redemptorist priest in 1950 whom Paisley rebuked as an idolater. He was Father Arthurs from Clonard; a gentle, loving soul coming to my various needs when, as a mixed-up teenager at wits end corner, the 'saved' kept me at their doors, offering me little more than a brusque handshake with an "every blessing from the Lord"

In that humble, unassuming Redemptorist priest I saw the true radiance and reflection of a John the Divine! I have a whole volume of Dr Paisley's sermons but the way Father Arthur's, non-verbally, preached to me Christ was far superior to them all.

I wonder! How are WE preaching this gospel to every creature?

My Mummy is Dying, Pastor

When I was a Congregational minister in the early 1960s, a young girl of eleven approached me to visit her Mum, who had been given only a few weeks to live. I agreed, and on reaching the humble home in a back street of Barnsley, was hesitant as to what I should say. "Is it true that your life could be taken from you?" I asked. Tears filled the young mother's eyes as she lay in bed. She said her life hadn't always been good and that she could die at any time. She appeared terrified of death and of leaving her children.

For four years I'd studied pastoralia at a liberal seminary. How should I respond? Should I christen her in bed? Should I, with support from the deacons, speedily get her accepted in to Congregational church membership? Should I administer private communion to her? Or should I share some abstract speculation about, what lecturers had termed, 'the great unknown'?

I would not pile on the agony! In a flash I jettisoned the dry theology that had entrenched me for seven barren years. "It is not religion, but knowing Jesus who still lives that counts" I said, "Jesus is no respecter of people and you can know Him as well as the likes of Cliff Richard, Pat Boone, Roy Rogers and millions more. He died for all and comes into the lives of all who sincerely invite Him". That lovely distraught should, guided by me, there and then thanked the Lamb of God for dying in her place; asked Him to come into her life; and thanked Him for doing so.

Next Lord's Day the little girl made her way to church. "Pastor, you've made my mummy very happy", she said. "Will come and see her again?" I did. There was now a peace and serenity glowing from that mother's countenance and within a few days the Saviour took her to His home.

Later, I met the young girl's father. He shook his head from side to side. "I simply can't understand it. You took all fear from my wife. Instead of being afraid to die she actually seemed to be looking forward to it. I'd give the world to have her experience. "You may have it!" I said. You can have that same experience. It is a real encounter with the living Jesus she's had. Cliches such as 'being saved', 'born again', 'got converted', or 'seen the light', are inadequate and much abused terms expressive of that same dynamic experience". I spoke to him for some time, but the next time he avoided me as though I'd touched a raw nerve.

For better or worse, I was soon off to Oxford having transferred my allegiance to Anglicanism where the shackles of low church liberalism would be superseded by those of high church ritualism. I never saw that man again: but by God's grace, I will see his wife again! And, please God, *at least* his daughter also.

I am the voice of the voiceless
Through me the dumb will speak,
Till the deaf worlds ear be made to hear
The wrongs of the wordless weak

From street, from cage and from kennel,
From stable and zoo, the wail
Of my tortured kin proclaim the sin
Of the mighty against the frail

Oh, shame on the mothers of mortals
Who have not stopped to teach
Of the sorrow that lies in dear, dumb eyes
The sorrow that has no speech

The same force formed the sparrow
That fashioned man the king;
The God of the whole gave a spark of soul
To furred and feathered thing

And I am my brother's keeper,
And I will fight his fight
And speak the word for beast and bird,
Till the world shall set things right

Ella Wheeler Wilcox

Praise for Creatures Great and Small

Hymns and meditations concerning animals.
A compilation for pet services and private devotion.

Compiled by
Revd. James Thompson

Hymn	Author
All things asked we will receive	Paul H Berry
Creator God, you have conferred	Arthur R Day
Creator on high, we sing to your praise	Revd Mark Bishop
Creator Spirit, God most high	Miss C M Wilson
Dear Father God, we make a plea	Betty Swift
Dear Holy Spirit, tenderest of doves	Revd James Thompson
Dear Lord, accept the prayers we offer	Linda J Bodicoat
Faithful Master, feed me	Mrs M E Powell
Father, let us all remember	Mrs Paddy Phillips
Go tell all creatures in the world	Armorel Kay Walling
God gave a life of beauty	Miriam E Roberts
God made this earth for man to share	Liz Stanford
Here we bring our animals	Late Paula Graham
Holy Spirit, life divine	Revd James Thompson
If we could stumble under loads	Miss Christine Ralph
Let earth rejoice and heaven adore	Muriel Stammers MBE
O beasts lift up your voice	H Joan Chaplain
O Dear Father God	Betty Swift
O God of all creation	Barbara Deane
O Lord, Creator of us all	Anonymous
O Lord of earth and air and sea	Victorine Buttberg
O teach us Dear Father	Mrs Coral Williams
Oh, Master, who first gave us birth	Miss Sally S Brown
On land, in air, in sea we dwell	Mrs Winifred Clark
Spirit of Holiness	Revd James Thompson
The beasts and birds both wild and tame	Hazel E Carey
The pets we love were made by Thee	May C Jenkins
The shaggy dog alone and stray	Joyce Fraser
We pray, O Lord for blessing	H Joan Chaplain
We thank Thee Lord for wings and beaks	H Jack Stubbington
When Noah built the Ark	Mrs Brenda Trend

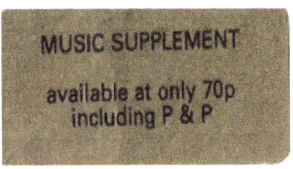

MUSIC SUPPLEMENT
available at only 70p
including P & P

PRAISE FOR CREATURES GREAT AND SMALL

'I' would ring the bells of Heaven
the greatest peel in years,
If parson lost his senses
and people came to theirs
And he and they together
knelt down with angry prayers
For poor, maimed, blind pit ponies,
dancing dogs and hunted hares

Ralph Hodgson 1871-1962

©1988 James Thompson
St. Clements Publications
Mastrick Drive
Aberdeen AB2 6UF

By Way of Introduction

How embracing is the love of the Christ! Yet, for many centuries the Jewish concept of God's benevolence was one confined to its own race. The criticism of many leading prophets was against this. They realised that their Nation which had been chosen to be the greatest of missionary nations often preferred to keep God's salvation exclusively to itself. Was that the message behind Jonah? Well thankfully we have come a long way; most people of God today believe that He is concerned about the whole human race.

But alas, we haven't yet travelled far enough, so many still fail to realise what far-off Jonah knew: God is concerned for cattle as well as Ninevites! Jonah 3:8 & 4:11). Everything that breathes is of concern to God and if our Faith does not encompass the birds. Beasts fish and insects, not to mention the flowers, the grass and the trees then our vision is indeed paltry. It hasn't evolved as far as those early prophets such as Isaiah whose dream was nothing short of a future golden age of glory, later referred to by some as a Millennial age, wherein Paradise would be more than restored through the labours of a second Adam.

Well, we who know Him; we who are Messiah's Sons and Daughters; let us seek to prepare the way. One way in which this can be wonderfully done is in fostering and furthering Services in which the whole of the animal creation is remembered. Indeed, for the sake of humanity alone, the practice of encouraging the young to pray for, as well as protect defenceless creatures, is a sure way to bring about a better order.

One might be forgiven for believing that if as much time had been spent in troubled Ulster instilling into the young the concepts of a Francis of Assisi rather than exclusiveness of religious factions then that land which borders on a bloodbath could have spiritually blossomed as the rose!

It is not wrong to make place for the animals within our worship; the early Celtic Church did it, and it was only with a later Aristotelian philosophy permeating Latin Christendom that animals began to be excluded from a concept of divine salvation. The evolving contemporary inclination to hold services in which people not only pray for, but actually bring their pets to Church, is not a departure but rather a return to that inclusiveness which was so apparent in those memorable Bible times.

Indeed, as early as Job, the prophet is conscious of animals recognising their Creator (Job 12:7-9) while later, Joel reminds us that when they cry to Him their needs are met (Joel 1:18-20 & 2:22). David himself recognises the Lord as Saviour of man and beast: (Psalm 36:6) and indeed, the supreme analogy concerning the depth of the Creator's love is vividly expressed in terms of a simple shepherd's care and concern for each of his flock. What a glowing testimony to such, often despised, peasant stock!

Then when Messiah came in the fullness of time, he aptly applied such a role as fulfilled in his dear self. So let us see to it that we, with the centuries of a post biblical Christendom behind us, do not fall into the frightful heresy of making our God too small. That first biblical covenant after the flood was with the whole of the creation (Genesis 9:16); 'Lord, forgive us the terrible sin of having left so much of it outside!'

* * * * * * * * * * *

The purpose of this book is two-fold. It is meant to be used as a companion for Christian Animal Services such as those recently commenced in Westminster Abbey, York Minster, St Giles and St Mary's in Edinburgh and Salisbury Cathedral; indeed, ten of the hymns contained were used in the former as well as some of the prayers (the result of a competition organised by myself and my friends Alison and Andre Johnson of Harris). However, a considerable number of other hymns have trickled in to me, equally as good and some better. This selection is largely the outcome: an aid towards holding an animal service be it in the Abbey, a Cathedral, a Parish Church of Anglican, Reformed or Episcopal tradition, or equally a glorious Chapel, Citadel, Mission or Assembly; not forgetting schools, rallies, house meetings; and the great "out of doors"!

To this end, scope and flexibility is allowed between preference for a non-liturgical meeting and a structured one. Such animal services are now "catching on" all over, and for those following a liturgical year, they are becoming increasingly popular on the second Sunday after Easter (Good Shepherd Sunday), as well as on the nearest Sunday to the feast of St Francis (the 4th October).

Such a compilation as this, however, is not confined to a possible twice-yearly public usage; it is clearly a devotional book to be used for private meditation and reflection. These hymns, as well as the readings and prayers, have each got a biblical message to impart. To the kind of question, "Do animals have a soul?" particularly to any who might have recently loved and lost one, here within this small volume you are discovering such an answer; and I sincerely believe that to be a blessing in itself. Back to the scriptures must be the quest of each evangelical (the Reformers and the Early Fathers are not enough!) and that is the path of the present writer.

Following on from this introduction are three sections of which the first is by far the largest: a truly varied yet selective choice of hymns to each of which is given a familiar or most appropriate tune (and for those preferring another, the metre is appended). There then follows an Order of Service which may be used admirably well in its entirety or, if preferred, modified. Then last of all there are a series of intercessions with further biblical passages both of which may be used for devotional study or as a useful help for any wishing to compile their own Order of Service. Lists of some reputable animal societies religious or otherwise are appended for prayer support.

The benefit of this publication when used at public worship means that the Order of Service can be adhered to and the hymns used by merely turning back the pages to sing the ones the minister or priest has chosen. Alternatively, the minister may prefer to be free of such a setting. He is then able to use the volume for congregation and self exclusively as a hymnal compiled for such a service. And indeed, in a eucharistic setting this will of necessity apply.

To meet the above variation of needs this publication has been prayerfully compiled. Rightfully used it will contribute to a service remarkably blest in every respect. Have no doubt about it that animals can be keenly aware of spiritual influences. They can even be exceedingly gracious when coming forward to the communion rail for a blessing. One would lift its paw upwards towards me as I lifted my arm in blessing towards it! And for those who are not too sure as to what kind of blessing to give a dumb creature at a communion rail, mercy seat or elsewhere, here is one you might well like to use; it comes most appropriately from a Revd Mr Good of Wakefield!

'Our Lord Jesus Christ, who was cradled amongst the beasts at his birth, and rode into Jerusalem upon an ass, bless you and all your kind, now and always'

Incidentally, regardless of Mark 16:18, one is hardly wise to bring down a hand of blessing on to the head of a dog that's over self-protective – sometimes because of past ill treatment. Indeed, an observable side approach to the face followed by stroking behind the ear is more commendable. But where there is any doubt a blessing from a distance will prove far more effective all round!

Those preparing for such a service need to see it that dishes of water are amply provided in appropriate spots. And unless animals are normally close to each other, then the more spaced out they are – and preferably away from any children who tease – then the more receptive they will be to the atmosphere of worship.

All told, you'll usually find the commotion (if any) far less distracting than one would normally expect to witness at an average Christening or dedication. And, regardless of what folk might anticipate, a visiting card is not normally left, though a shovel in the vestibule will certainly do no harm!!

James Thompson

HYMNS FOR ANIMALS

Hymn 1

1. Here we bring our animals to the King of Kings,
   We may have some large pets, some with tiny wings.
   This their day of blessing from the Heavenly Throne,
   Bless the Lord, protect them; and each and every home.

Chorus

   Here we bring our animals to the King of Kings
   Bless the Lord, protect them, help us love all things.

2. In the Jungle Forests, may they live with pride,
   Please, dear Lord, protect them so they need not hide
   Let us be united in our love for them,
   Help us teach all others, not their lives condemn.

Chorus

3. God provided Noah an Ark, animals two by two,
   To ride the stormy waters, saved for me and you;
   And like good Saint Francis, who loved them every one,
   We must help and care for them; until their life spans done.

Chorus

4. And we bring ourselves dear Lord, help us in our work,
   May our efforts shine Lord, may no shadows lurk.
   Bless our animal helpers here, in their daily tasks,
   Guide them in decisions is the prayer we all would ask.

Chorus

Written by the late Paula Graham – RSPCA
Could be sung to 'St Gertrude' (6.5.6.5. Ter.)

Hymn 2

1. Let earth rejoice and heaven adore
   The great Creator's works to see,
   Whose Holy Word and Wisdom caused
   The new-made heaven and earth to be.

2. He, who for human-kind decreed
   Over all creatures to hold sway,
   Gave through His Son a greater charge –
   We should the rule of love obey.

3. Spirit of God, who saw with joy
   All that was made and called it good,
   Grant us true wisdom that we may
   Seek without sin our daily food.

4. O Trinity, whose matchless power
   For freedom framed the human will
   Give human hands the power to serve
   And not to injure, maim and kill.

5. So shall the glorious works of God
   Praise Him with glad united voice
   And all that Love and Wisdom made
   On Earth adore, in Heaven rejoice.

Written by Miss Muriel Stanmere MBE
Could be sung to 'Fulda' (L.M.)

Hymn 3

1. Spirit of holiness above,
   Who madest all we so much love
   Descend upon us in this hour,
   Each creature here to feel Thy power.

2. Bless every animal we bring,
   That they with us Thy praise shall sing
   The dumb in deeper depth express,
   The oral prayers of our mankind.

3. Make us aware, like Balsam's ass,
   When angels cross before our path
   Grant us the eyes that we might see,
   Horses and chariots sent by Thee.

4. Give us the lion's courage now;
   With it the meekness of the lamb
   That with discernment sought from Thee,
   We 'in Christ's Name' shall take each stand.

5. Grant us the calmness of the dove,
   A donkey felt with Christ above
   That in the roar of crowds around,
   We too in peace may still be found.

6. Take from us narrowness and pride,
   Man's false theology that's lied
   Until with creatures whom we love,
   We sing Thy praises joined above.

Written by the Revd. James Thompson
Could be sung to 'Deep Harmony' (L.M.)

Hymn 4

1. When Noah built the Ark,
   So long ago in time,
   He gathered up the animals.
   And out them in a line

Chorus

   Oh! Abba you're the Shepherd,
   Of creatures great and small,
   So loving and so trusting,
   Protect and bless them all.

2. There were two of them of each kind,
   All creatures great and small,
   So loving and so trusting,
   Protect and bless them all.

Chorus

3. Skies of black and so much lightening,
   That came from God on High,
   Rains and thunder was so frightening,
   Forty days and nights went by

Chorus

4. The rains did cease, and Noah –
   He did release a dove,
   And Almighty God sent a rainbow down,
   In His everlasting love,

Chorus

Written by Mrs Brenda Trend. Could be sung to 'The Holly and the Ivy' (Irregular)

Hymn 5

1. Creator Spirit, God most High,
   When all was cold and dark and void,
   You made the light and warmth and land,
   And diverse creatures great and small.
   The birds and beasts You brought to birth
   To share with man this kindly earth.

2. Oh Christ whose careful eye discerned
   The fox's hole, the shepherd's flock,
   And sparrows twittering in the dust
   All compassed by a Father's Love,
   When palms and shouts were raised on high
   You on a colt came riding by.

3. With Israel's prophet who foretold
   The lion dwelling with the Lamb,
   With psalmist asking praises due
   From coney and Leviathan,
   With Francis, Lord we make our prayer
   That for Your Creatures we may care!

Written by Miss C M Wilson
Could be sung to 'Melita' (88.88.88)

Hymn 6

1. Oh Lord, Creator of us all
   We give our thanks to thee
   For all our pets both large and small
   How grateful we should be!

2. Pray help us give the kindly care
   That they all need from us,
   For it is only right and fair
   That we should treat them thus

3. And when they show by love and trust
   How faithful they can be,
   It makes one feel that try we must
   To put more faith in Thee.

4. Again, Oh Lord, we pray for all
   Thy creatures living rough,
   For they have neither bed nor stall
   And life for them is tough.

5. One day we hope that this will cease
   And happiness will reign,
   The wolf and lamb will dwell in peace
   And suffer no more pain.

"Anonymous"
Could be sung to 'Horsley' or 'Irish' (C.M.)

Hymn 7

1. Creator on high, we sing to your praise;
   You moulded all life, in countless wise ways.
   You made every creature for land, sea, and air;
   To all humankind you entrusted their care.

2. Our Saviour paid heed to all living things;
   The animals' friend, yet true King of Kings.
   He needed a donkey for humble display,
   And showed His concern for the sheep gone astray.

3. O God of all life, may animals know,
   We work for their good; help friendship to grow.
   The eyes of all creatures look upward to you;
   Lord, make us your agents in all we can do.

4. The pets that we keep, the beasts on the farm,
   You wish us to tend, and keep them from harm,
   Lord, reverence for life may we learn from above;
   So bind us, with Nature, together in love.

Written by the Revd. Mark Bishop
Could be sung to 'Hanover' (55.55.65.65)

Hymn 8

1. Dear Lord, accept the prayers we offer,
   For all Thy creatures in our care.
   That none may suffer fear and violence,
   Your guiding hand be always there.

2. For each and every humble sparrow,
   Our Master marks their single fall.
   Teach us to strive, and never weaken
   The tireless fight to save them all.

3. Give us a heart of tender mercy,
   Let no wild beast in suffering lie.
   For them eternal freedom granted,
   By hunters gun no more shall die.

4. Far round the world this prayer is offered
   For strength and guidance from above,
   Make us aware of all their suffering,
   And keep them in your wondrous love.

Written by Linda J Bodicoat
Could be sung to 'St Clement' (9.8.9.8)

Hymn 9

1. O teach us Dear Father
   Creator of all
   Respect for your creatures
   The great and the small
   O give us compassion
   And help us to care
   For all forms of Life
   On this planet we share.

2. Lord help us protect them
   Your flocks and your herds
   For they will not suffer
   If we heed your words
   The trapped and the hunted
   The frightened and meek
   Lord teach us to help them
   The dumb and the weak.

3. Lord make us remember
   Their value and worth
   We're all equal members
   Of your precious earth
   You gave your dominion
   To our human race
   O give us the wisdom
   To use it with grace

Written by Mrs Coral Williams
Could be sung to 'St Denio' (11.11.11.11.)

Hymn 10

1. God made this Earth for Man to share
   With all the other creatures He'd put there
   But we've abused His just and mighty plan
   Believing Planet Earth was just for man
   > God's chosen beasts of land and air and sea
   > We must protect to keep them wild and free
   > Give them our love as God has surely done
   > And dwell upon this Earth as one.

2. In tortured pain some meet their fate
   Unfeeling Vivisectors lie in wait
   For those that have no voice – we must unite
   Bring Justice to their sad and sorry plight
   > Hunters must be thwarted from their chase
   > The sea, for whales, must be a safer place
   > To raise the Cross of Pain these creatures bear
   > We'll have to fight to prove we care.

3. Our Great Creator high above
   Must surely weep to see Man's selfish love
   For creatures of the farm should still be free
   Days for shooting game should never be
   > So listen well to me, my Fellow-Man
   > And join us now in doing what you can
   > To make our Planet Earth a finer place
   > So Love will lead the Human Race.

4. God made this Earth for Man to share
   With all the other creatures He's put there
   To make our Planet Earth a finer place
   So Love will lead the Human Race.

Written by Liz Stanford
Could be sung to – Make me a channel: St Francis

Hymn 11

1. Go tell all creatures in the world
   The Good News that I bring;
   That was the message Jesus gave,
   And He is Lord and King.

2. Let's tell it by the deeds we do;
   In ways they don't understand:
   Deal gently with the beasts and birds
   Who share our Saviour's land.

3. Protect His forests, heal the air,
   Care for His shining sea,
   Arrest our cruelty and greed
   And sets its victims free.

4. So shall our lives proclaim the One
   Who sent a little child
   To lead all things safe home, in Him
   Redeemed and reconciled.

5. To where – upon His holy hill –
   None hurt and none destroy
   And all Creation's present groans
   Are turned to songs of joy.

   Amen

Written by Armorel Kay Walling
Could be sung to 'St Fulbert' (C.M.)

Hymn 12

1. Creator God, you have conferred
   On fallible humanity
   Dominion over beast and bird
   And all that moves on land and sea;
   Lord, help us ever to recall
   You made them all, you love them all

2. The stabled cattle first adored
   The new-born Christ on Christmas morn,
   And on a donkey was the Lord
   Triumphant to his passion borne;
   God, living on the earth he made,
   Scorn'd not those humble creatures' aid.

3. But humans in their vanity
   Assume the world to be their own,
   And with their mindless cruelty
   They make the whole creation groan;
   Lord, help us ever to recall
   You made all creatures great and small.

4. For all your creatures make us care,
   Impatience help us to restrain,
   Rememb'ring that with us they share
   Our need of love, our fear and pain,
   And grant us skill and gentleness
   To succour them when in distress

5. Bring near, O Lord, that perfect day
   Of loving-kindness, peace and joy,
   When non shall on another prey
   And none shall injure or destroy.
   And in a world from sin set free
   All creatures live in harmony.

Written by Arthur R Day. Could be sung to 'Melita' (88.88.88)

Hymn 13

1. We thank Thee Lord for wings and beaks,
    For paws and wagging tails.
    For worms and slugs and centipedes,
    For flies and bees and snails.

2. We oft forget that we are one,
    Thy life is in us all
    And they as well as black and white
    Are subject to Thy law.

3. We claim dominion. They just live
    Accepting all Thy grace
    And man forgets and turns aside
    And fails to see Thy face.

4. In cat or dog or cow or sheep.
    Remind us Lord above
    That what we sow, we'll also reap
    Of hate as well as love.

5. So whether two feet, four, or none
    With fins or shell or sting
    We'll praise Thee Lord and shower our care
    On every living thing.

Written by H. Jack Stubbington
Could be sung to 'Lloyd' (C.M.)

Hymn 14

1. All things asked we will receive
   That His promise we believe
   So we ask our Lord above
   To include the pets we love.

2. Those who seek will always find
   Their own Shepherd who's so kind
   Such a pattern should teach us
   True respect for all creatures

3. Love thy neighbour must imply
   All that's in the earth and sky
   That's a duty that infers
   More care for the Universe.

4. So with this example clear
   Help to promote love not fear
   Till we see Him, who was slain,
   When we too rise up again.

Written by Paul H. Berry
Could be sung to 'Buckland' (7.7.7.7.)

Hymn 15

1. O God of all creation
   Of earth and sky and sea,
   O Lord of our Salvation
   We raise our eyes to Thee.
   We gaze in awe and wonder
   On all Thy gifts sublime,
   But in our hearts we ponder
   On man's abuse and crime.

2. We watch the might ocean
   Pound over rock and sand,
   We see the trees in motion
   Respond to wind's command.
   The mountains, plains and rivers,
   The ever-changing skies,
   Reflect God's love, the Giver
   Of Life that never dies.

3. We see His wondrous creatures
   With whom we share this earth,
   Their varied forms and features
   God given at their birth.
   The mighty whale, the firefly,
   The lion and the dove,
   The creatures of the night sky
   Watched o'er by God above.

4. But greed of man and nation
   Imposing its own law,
   Creating devastation
   With poison, axe and saw.
   His creatures maimed and broken
   By scalpel, fire and knife,
   Each death a bitter token
   Of man's disdain for life.

5. O God, when comes Thy kingdom
   When hate's replaced by love,
   When all life joins to sing then
   With those who dwell above?
   At that great celebration
   All creatures Thou wilt raise,
   And then, Lord, all creation
   Shall echo to Thy praise.

Written by Barbara Deane
Could be sung to 'Aurelia' (7.6.7.6.D)

Hymn 16

1. O dear Father God,
   Look down from above,
   Send Angels of light
   All clothed in your love,
   To seek out dark corners,
   Where animals wait
   Forsaken, forgotten
   Awaiting their fate.

2. O may all those men,
   Who cause so much pain,
   Be filled with such love,
   That never again,
   Will harm and destruction
   Be their shameful deed,
   Let love be their master
   And kindness their creed.

3. O Father of love
   Hear us as we pray
   Your creatures need help
   Each hour of the day
   We ask your direction
   So please be our guide
   To care and sustain them,
   Till they reach your side.

Written by Betty Swift
Could be sung to 'Hanover' (10.10.11.11.)

Hymn 17

1. The pets we love were made by Thee,
   As were the creatures wild
   The birds, in cage or flying free
   Delight both man and child.

2. The dogs and cats inspire our love,
   Our lives they gladly share.
   The dog can also serve us well –
   He leads the blind with care.

3. Affection goes to rabbits too
   And guinea-pigs give joy.
   Hamsters and gerbils are beloved
   By many a girl and boy.

4. They merit care as well as love
   And we should know their need –
   And so ensure these gifts of Thine
   From grief and pain are freed.

Written by May C. Jenkins
Could be sung to 'Kings Langley' (C.M.)

Hymn 18

1. We pray, O Lord, for blessing
   On all remembered here,
   The beasts of farm and woodland,
   And pets whom we hold dear;
   For hunted fox and badger,
   For otter, pheasant, hare,
   Ill-treated horse and donkey
   Who have no proper care.

2. O stir our conscience strongly
   To stop experiment
   On dogs and cats and rabbits,
   For those on beauty bent;
   O spare these lives so harmless
   Who die for human gain,
   And give them peace from suffering,
   Release them from their pain.

3. We pray for all the seal pups
   So cruelly clubbed to death
   While gazing at their killers
   With trust, to their last breath;
   O make men feel compassion
   For all created life,
   So we and your creation
   Shall be no more at strife.

Written by H. Joan Chaplin
Could be sung to 'Aurelia' (7.6.7.6.D.)

.

Hymn 19

1. If we could stumble over loads,
   Like Beasts of burden everywhere,
   Or feel the sharp and painful goads,
   'Let men desist' would be our prayer.

2. If we were hunted, maimed, or killed,
   Though not at fault, nor knowing why,
   Or close confined, our vigour stilled,
   'Let men desist' would be our cry.

3. If we were birds and kept encaged,
   Our only longing to be free,
   Would not all thinkers be enraged?
   'Let men desist' would be our plea.

4. But we are men – we cause the pain,
   We kill and maim, blind and destroy.
   May God our senseless ways restrain,
   And let His world live for our joy.

Written by Miss Christine Ralph
Could be sung to 'Angels Song', 'Breslaw',
or 'Tallis Canon' (L.M.)

Hymn 20

1. The shaggy dog alone and stray,
   No-one to love or to obey.
   He walks the streets, no-one to greet,
   The Lord alone He cares for you.

2. The tabby cat whose time is nigh,
   For if no food you'll surely die.
   Your skin so thin, your legs so weak
   The Lord alone He cares for you.

3. So come with me you tabby cat,
   And lay your head upon my lap.
   And shaggy dog lay by my side,
   The Lord and I will care for you.

Written by Joyce Fraser
Could be sung to 'Williams' (L.M.)

Hymn 21

1. God gave a life of beauty
   To our dear planet earth
   He planted seeds in plenty
   With power to bring re-birth.
   He set the plan in motion
   For rivers to run free.
   All nature trusts His wisdom –
   Then why, oh why can't we?

Chorus

    All nature is Your Kingdom,
   And we are partners too.
   In full and glad allegiance
   We will be true to You.

2. He made the feathered song birds,
   And taught them in their ways
   Of how to feed their nestlings,
   And how to sing His praise.
   The eagles build their eyrie,
   We wrens nest in a tree.
   Yes, birds obey His ruling –
   Then why, oh why won't we?

Chorus

3. Creator God, You tendered
         Creation for our care
   All pets and farmyard creatures,
   All wildlife in their lair,
   You fashioned living matter
   To live dependently
   On others in your Kingdom.
   The why, oh why can't we?

Chorus

4. The Lord said, "Have dominion
   O'er bird and beast and land."
   Man's duty with such honour must
   Be guided by His hand.
   Beasts gently serve their masters,
   And live obediently.
   They serve a living Saviour –
   Then why, oh why don't we?

Chorus

Written by Miriam E. Roberts
Could be sung to 'Dresden'
(7.6.7.6.D. & Refrain)

Hymn 22

1. O beasts lift up your voice,
   You sad and patient crowd,
   From factory pen, and battery cage,
   Cry out your wrongs aloud.

2. From badger, fox and hare
   The cry goes up "How long
   Must we be hunted to our death,
   The weak killed by the strong?"

3. The whales and seals die, too,
   To satisfy men's greed,
   O when shall men see God made all,
   And help them in their need?

4. We pray your Kingdom come,
   A time of peace for all;
   For each ill-treated animal
   O please God hear our call.

Written by H. Joan Chaplin
Could be sung to 'Carlisle' (S.M.)

Hymn 23

1. Holy Spirit, life divine
   Broaden Thou this soul of mine
   Show me creatures great and small
   How they follow at Thy call,

2. Holy Spirit, precious dove
   Make within me nought but love
   Then dumb creatures will not be
   Frightened by the likes of me

3. Holy Spirit, Lord of peace
   Make all strife and struggles cease,
   May each creature live to be
   Sanctified and blest in Thee.

4. Holy Spirit who dost care
   May all creatures learn to share.
   Take from man his haughty trait
   That at last he might see straight.

5. Holy Spirit, Lord of fire
   May Thy servants never tire
   Burning bright for dumb and all
   Till evil systems break and fall.

6. Holy Spirit, at the last
   With all pain and travail past
   May all creatures join-ed be
   In the Sanctus offered Thee.

Written by the Revd. James Thompson
Could be sung to 'Harts' (7.7.7.7.)

Hymn 24

1. Oh, Mater, who first gave us birth
   And all things living on this earth
   Appointed Thou our lowly place
   To serve and feed the human race.
   'Creator hearken to our plea
   Protect us from man's cruelty.'

2. It seems our portion to provide
   Our milk and flesh and often hide
   We pray for kin so cruelly slain
   By matadors all over Spain.
   'Oh hearken to our bovine plea
   Protect us from man's cruelty.'

3. In tiny boxes two foot square
   Deprived of sunlight and fresh air
   We cast in the collecting tray
   The eggs we must provide each day.
   'Oh hearken to our avian pleas
   Release us from captivity.'

4. Oh Lord, You surely never meant
   To use us for experiments
   We, who are sent lost sheep to find,
   To sniff out drugs and lead the blind.
   'Oh hearken to our canine plea
   Protect us from man's cruelty.'

Written by Miss Sally S. Brown
Could be sung to 'St Catherine' or 'Melita' (88.88.88)

Hymn 25

1. Father, let us all remember
   Every animal You made.
   Fish and fur and bird and reptile
   Figure in Your Grand Parade.
   Grant us patience, understanding.
   Let compassion never fade.

2. Father, let us stop all cruelty,
   May we follow in Your wake.
   We must help them for they need us.
   Show us Lord, the path to take.
   Might we always fight their cause and
   Love all creatures for Your sake.

3. Father, let us give them justice.
   Grant that there will be one day
   Love and trust through all Creation,
   No more fear, and that we may
   Treat all animals with kindness.
   We shall learn You are the Way

Written by Mrs Paddy Phillips
Could be sung to 'Mannheim' (87.87.87.)

Hymn 26

1. The beasts and birds both wild and tame
   From meadow plain and hill;
   In mute appeal their God acclaim
   His purpose to fulfil.

2. "We were His creatures first of all
   Before He made a man,
   But men rule now, are we in thrall,
   No longer in His plan?

3. Dependant on the human race
   For our concern and care,
   God send them wisdom, love and grace,
   That we may better fare.

4. Our lives are often spent in toil
   Or shortened for men's use;
   Yet to our masters we are loyal
   Though prey to their misuse.

5. Lighten our way that we may share
   This world we called our own
   With humans who have learnt to care
   For creatures wild and known

Written by Hazel E Carey
Could be sung to 'St Peter' (C.M.)

Hymn 27

1. On land, in air, in sea, we dwell,
   Within Thy tender care.
   We do our best to aid and serve,
   This world that we all share.

2. Oh hear, dear Lord, our heartfelt prayer,
   That man will hear your words,
   And teach his Lord like You to care
   For Animals and Birds.

3. His food and raiment we provide
   And serve him in our way.
   We do not ask for wealth or power,
   Just kindness day by day.

4. We cannot speak with tongues of man,
   Man thinks of us as dumb.
   But Thou, dear Lord, can read our thoughts,
   To Thee in hope we come.

5. When all our worldly toils are o'er
   At Thy right hand we'll meet,
   And Animal and Man at last,
   Will worship at Thy feet.

Written by Mrs Winifred Clark
Could be sung to 'Belmont' (C.M.)

Hymn 28

1. Oh Lord of earth and air and sea,
   Dear is the life Thou gavest me;
   Free was I born, pray keep me free,
   Who madest all.

2. Beneath the starlight's gentle ray,
   Humble my birth on bed of hay;
   The Son of God thus lowly lay,
   When He was born.

3. He came to wash man's sins away,
   To teach him kindness day by day,
   That we might live a better way,
   As brothers all.

4. But evil men heard not His word,
   They sought to kill by stone and sword;
   Upon a cross they nailed the Lord
   Who came to save.

5. Soften men's hearts my life to spare,
   Save me from gin-trap and from snare,
   Keep me, Creator, in Thy care,
   Who lovest all.

Written by Victorine Buttberg
Could be sung to 'Almsgiving' (8.8.8.4.)

Hymn 29

Chorus Faithful Master, feed me,
    I am your loyal friend,
    Faithful Master, love me,
    As I will to the end.

1. Each day I try to greet you
   Whenever you come home,
   I try to guard the house too,
   Whenever left alone. (Chorus)

2. I am your loyal servant
   And do as I am told,
   I know it is not easy
   Because I'm growing old. (Chorus)

3. God gave us time together,
   Such happy times were they,
   He said we'd stay together
   Until I'm called away. (Chorus)

4. But, now I thank Him dearly
   For all that He has done
   To make my life so happy,
   With You, it's been such fun. (Chorus)

5. When I am called to Heaven,
   I'll still remember you,
   The hand that always fed me,
   And gave me comfort too.
   Faithful Master, feed me,
   Spare me your kindly hand,
   Faithful Master, love me,
   My time is at an end.

Written by Mrs M E Powell.
Could be sung to 'All things bright and beautiful' (7.6.7.6. & Refrain)

Hymn 30

1. Dear Father God we make a plea,
   For creatures made by Thee,
   That man will know and understand
   They too share this our land.

2. Each furry friend with eyes so bright,
   Cringe not from us in fright,
   But know that we a friend should be
   Through all eternity.

3. Let no wild animal be found
   With caging all around,
   But roaming where they ought to be –
   In freedom, just like me.

4. May all creatures chased for sport,
   And those in traps so caught,
   Suffer no more, or feel such pain,
   Let love and kindness reign.

5. May we all think before we buy –
   So many have to die,
   There is sufficient for our need,
   But not for all the greed.

6. We ask for cruelty to cease,
   And each one to have peace,
   That peace which comes from You above
   Perfect, and lasting love.

Written by Betty Swift
Could be sung to 'Richmond' (C.M.)

Hymn 31

1. Dear Holy Spirit, tenderest of doves,
   Make me to love creatures as You do above
   Give me compassion more than just for man
   That I Your world might fully span.

2. Your covenant was not confined to man
   Creatures who worship are also in Your plan
   Save us from heresies that keep them out
   Man's pomp, his pride and scriptural doubt.

3. Teach me to know that Jesus died for all
   God's second Adam to counteract the fall
   That Paradise, once lost, be more than won
   Where creatures joint to praise the Son.

4. Teach us to know that what man sows he'll reap
   To wilfully harm is to sink within that deep
   There to remain true victim of their crime
   No Lamb of God on them to shine.

5. For the creation travailing in pain
   Seeking from us some protection to obtain
   Make Sons of God co-workers in Your plan
   Restoring all, and not just man.

6. Bring Lord the day when barriers shall break
   Fruits of our caring, as dogmas we forsake
   Then shall compassion all this Globe embrace
   We, with our pets, behold Your face.

Written by the Revd. James Thompson
Could be sung to 'Holly' (L.M.)

An Order of Worship

Providing seven brief meditations and allowing for relevant singing. Readers (not forgetting young and old!) could be responsible for a passage numbered, or prayer which follows.

———————

Choice of Introductory Sentences – Calls of Worship

MINISTER: And I will make a covenant for you with the beasts of the field, the fowls of the air, and the creeping things of the ground....
And you will lie down in safety (Hosea 2:18) And Jesus was with the wild beasts as the angels ministered to him. (Mark 1:13)

O how amiable are Thy dwellings, Lord of Hosts! The sparrow has found herself a house, and the swallow a nest where she may lay her young; even Thine altars, O Lord of hosts, my King and my God. (Psalm 84)

Are not two sparrows sold for one farthing, yet not one falls to the ground except your Father knows of it. (Matthew 10:29)

A righteous man cares for the needs of his beast (Proverbs 12:10). He shall feed his flock like a shepherd; he shall gather the lambs with his arm, and carry them in his bosom, and gently lead those that are with young. (Isaiah 40:11)

MINISTER: Opening Hymn

1ˢᵗ READING   (Genesis 9:8-17)

pause to recollect –

LET US PRAY
Lord God of Heaven and earth, You care for the whole of Your creation and not just for man's part within it.

When the waters assuaged you made your covenant with us all. You gave the beautiful rainbow not only as a sign to man but also to bird, beast and every living creature. Never again will you flood this world!

You who brought the whole of creation inside your covenant, forgive man for striving to put all forms of life, except his own, outside of it.

For Jesus' sake we ask it. Amen.

| Or* | Lord in your mercy |
| (response) | Hear our prayer |

2ⁿᵈ READING   (Numbers 22:21-35)

-pause to recollect-

LET US PRAY:
Father, God in a brutal world where man exploits the dumb and defenceless creation, save us from the callousness of Balaam!

Teach us to realise that many an animal spiritually perceives what man in his blindness fails to see – an angel sent from God.

*If congregational responses are not the norm, the first ending prevails throughout; if they are, the second prevails consistently.

Take away from the animals their fear of us, because they perceive not fiends to destroy them but rather friends to deliver them.

For Jesus' sake we ask it. Amen.

OR	Lord in your mercy
(response)	Hear our prayer.

———————

MINISTER: Hymn

———————

3rd READING   (Isaiah 11:1-9)

                             -pause to recollect-

LET US PRAY

Gracious God, when Messiah reigns and Paradise is more than restored, Your creatures will no longer prey upon each other, but play with each other instead! No more will anything strong be carnivorous. But compassionate. The Meek One will lead by his faithfulness instead of the mighty their force. Help us then, to turn our topsy turvy standards right side up, that should the Christ child return we may accept His leadership.

For Jesus' sake we as it, Amen.

OR   Lord in your mercy

             Hear our prayer.

4th READING   (John 10: 1-16)

                             -pause to recollect-

LET US PRAY:

Father, we thank you for the character of those biblical shepherds; a character perceived by timid sheep, so that when they heard their shepherd's cry, rather than scatter for safety, they immediately followed for refuge.

We thank you for those men who acted as a very door of protection into the sheep pen; resting there at night so that no hostile creature could attack the fold, except over their very body!

We thank you because those herdsmen were prepared, if need be, to forfeit their lives to protect the flock. So noble was the character of a good shepherd that your Son used them as the supreme analogy of His love for us. No wonder you sent angels to <u>them</u> to tell of the birth of your Son!

Father, herdsmen seem to have altered so very much to what they were. If it be possible, make them again an analogy of your love.

For Jesus' sake we ask it. Amen.

OR	Lord in your mercy
(response)	Hear our prayer

MINISTER: Hymn

5th READING   (Mark 11:1-11)

-pause to recollect-

LET US PRAY:

Father, your son freed a donkey and brought it under His control; an ass that had never been ridden before was broken in without a murmur! The creature was then encircled by a hysterical mob who threw garments before it; broken branches were waved before its very eyes; shouting and shrieking before its ears. It bolted not, and Jesus gently guided its steps upwards to Jerusalem.

Teach us to realise that the calm in the midst of commotion, which Jesus imparted to that donkey, He is able to impart to us as well. May we hand over _our_ stubborn obstinate wills to your Son, that He may gently lead us to your Jerusalem above!

For Jesus' sake we ask it. Amen.

OR	Lord in your mercy
(response)	Hear our prayer'

6ᵗʰ READING   (Romans 8:18-22)

-pause to recollect-

LET US PRAY:
Father, this passage reminds us of others too! The world is not as you originally made it. You put man little lower than the angels, yet he rebelled against you and is now out of line with the rest of life. Man's sin has resulted in suffering – his dis-ease has affected the whole of creation, and what was once law and order is largely chaos and confusion.

Yet you love the culprit! You sent Jesus to rectify the wrong that man has done. As Paradise was lost, and the whole of creation suffers because of man's sin, so we learn that the whole of creation will benefit from man's salvation; and a greater Paradise will be reborn than that which was lost.

But how long must the dumb creation groan? How long must these labour pangs last before such a millennium arrives? O Lord help us to actualise such an era: show us how best to liberate captive creatures; how to speak for the dumb creation. Happily, they might then confirm us to be what we've so long confessed to be, "the sons of God!"

For Jesus' sake we ask it. Amen.

OR	Lord in your mercy
(response)	Hear our prayer.

MINISTER: Hymn

7ᵗʰ READING   (Revelation 4:2-11)

-pause to recollect-

LET US PRAY:

Dear God, as we behold the greatest Sanctuary of all, we learn that man does not approach it alone: other creatures are there as well!

Your rainbow arch surrounds You there – the symbol of Your covenant with every living creature.

For animal-like creatures lead their human counterparts in offering to You the greatest sanctus of all!

Lord, save us from human pride and vanity; the haughty spirit that excludes others from Your presence, or confines pride of place for one's self and one's own breed!

For Jesus' sake we ask it. Amen.

OR	Lord in your mercy
(response)	Hear our prayer.

MINISTER: Hymn

(If no sermon to follow then animals are brought forward to be blest during same).

SERMON (followed by hymn (during which the animals are blest).

INTERCESSIONS for any absent animals, especially the sick, stray or misused (could be mentioned by name; and followed by a short pause).

MINISTER: Closing Hymn (a collection could be taken for an appropriate charity. See end of book).

BENEDICTION

Intercessions and Prayers for Animals

The response given by all after each petition:*

"Let everything that has breath praise the Lord!"

WE THANK YOU GOD:

1. That no matter how they suffer, the animals are always remembered by You.

2. That animal, bird sanctuaries and hospitals have been established in many places and that many seabirds are being rescued from oil pollution.

3. That more doctors are turning to and supporting, medical research which does not use animals.

4. For all who are labouring to secure legislation for better treatment of dumb creatures.

5. For the earnest intentions of so many who are striving to found a true and righteous Peace on earth in which the animals will not be ignored or forgotten.

6. For the people who are giving their time, talents and money for the furtherance of animal welfare, especially for new work and new workers in many countries.

7. For the work of compassionate vets and others in animal dispensaries.

*Willing members of congregation could be responsible for reading a petition,

8. For the increase and success of Alternative medicine which will have no part in animal experimentation.

9. For those who bring cases of cruelty and hardship to the notice of the public via the Press, the screen and Christlike protests or demonstrations.

10. For the increase of Christian animal welfare associations and all reputable animal welfare societies. **Amen**

Make us all to be true neighbours and friends of the animal creation, and so more worthy followers of the Lord Jesus Christ.

INTERCESSIONS

TO THE CREATOR

Lord, teach me to look at all I see around me as your creation. Let me never forget that the same God who made me made the whole world and all the animals that are in it. Give me the grace to love all your creatures, for the sake of my Lord and Saviour, Jesus Christ, who has redeemed me on the cross. Amen.

John Henry Newman

At the close of each prayer following may be said:

    V: Lord in your mercy R: Hear our prayer

Or   V: Lord hear us R: Lord graciously hear us

TO THE FATHER

Eternal Father, source of life and light,

Whose love extends to all people, all creatures, all things;

Grant us true reverence for life which becomes those who believe in you,

Lest we despise it, degrade it, or come callously to destroy it.

Robert Runcie

TO THE SON

Glorious Christ, whose analogy was that of a Good Shepherd, make us more like yourself, so that we may express towards the dumb creation as much compassion and care as did humble shepherds who lived before you died. Shame us for our lack of sensitivity and care. Teach us who boast of Calvary to know we are not the whole of the world for which you suffered. Take the blindness from our eyes, the prejudice from our minds and the haughtiness from our hearts.

Save us from the arrogance which makes your love far too small, confining it to our own species just as your children once confined it to their own race. Make us aware of the fact that what we sow will inevitably reap, for we are all interdependent upon each other and your moral laws can never be traversed with impunity.

Lord grant that even the air which surrounds us may give out from us vibrations of love and trust, so that all animals will recognise in us the manifestation of your children.

Lord, accept this prayer, and make us all kind under-shepherds. We ask this for your name's sake.

James Thompson

TO THE HOLY SPIRIT

O blessed Spirit of God, grant that we might ever manifest the trait of two creatures with which Jesus was compared. Give us, like Him, the strength of the lion in denouncing heinous villains and the gentleness of the lamb in comforting helpless victims. In our endeavour to liberate the captives take from us all fear of man, but take not from us the spirit of sensitivity. Give us a skin thicker than that of any rhinoceros and beneath it a heart softer than any flesh.

Holy Spirit of God, make us bold as John the Baptist and as meek as John the Beloved. Give us nothing less than the balance of Jesus: the discernment to know when to portray the features of the lion, and when the features of the lamb.

Holy Spirit of God, do these things: anoint us afresh and use us from this day on to Your Glory and that of your whole creation.

James Thompson

TO THE DUMB CREATION

"We beseech Thee O Lord, to hear our supplications on behalf of the dumb creation who, after their kind, bless, praise and magnify Thee forever. Grant that all cruelty may cease out of our land; and deepen our thankfulness to Thee for the faithful companionship of those whom we delight to call our friends"

Written for the RSPCA Centenary celebrations

ANIMAL CHRISTIAN CONCERN PRAYER

O God, whose name is Love, you created this world and all that is in it. We ask you to look with compassion and mercy upon us all.

LORD, IN YOUR MERCY, HEAR OUR PRAYER (after each paragraph)

Look upon the companion animals, O God, which share our homes and our lives, and which show us a love and loyalty few men can surpass. Bless them for the pleasure and companionship they give, and protect all those who suffer neglect and cruelty.

Look, especially, O God, upon all those creatures which suffer at the hands of man in laboratories, intensive farms, abattoirs, traps, sport and entertainment. Be with them in their fear, pain and suffering, and hold them in your loving hands.

Look upon man, O God, your supreme creation, with love and mercy. Forgive us our selfishness and our cruelty and lead us gently back into your way of love. Transform our hearts until they truly reflect the way shown to us by your beloved son, Jesus Christ, whose love was perfect and who loved to the end that He gave his own life for us.

Forgive us our bitterness against those who abuse your creation, for Christ taught us to forgive, even as he forgave. Yet change the hearts of all who use animals with cruelty so that they may be filled with your love and mercy. Inspire all governments, and those in authority, to change the directions of medical research and food production, and to bring an end by law to all animal abuse.

Guide us, O God, by your Holy Spirit into his transforming way of truth and love, and nurture in us a Christ-like spirit of compassion which is boundless and perfect.

O God, we await the coming of your Kingdom, in our hearts and in your world.

Merciful Father, accept these prayers for the sake of your Son, our Saviour Jesus Christ.

May Tripp

FOR THE PROTECTION OF NATURE

"We thank thee, O God, for the joy in nature, for the play of the young, the vigour of the mature, the survival of creatures that are fitted to be happy. We pray that thou wilt lead all men to deal wisely and mercifully with thy birds and beasts and creeping things, as stewards who must answer to thee for their trust; to be considerate in their use of those that serve their wants, and compassionate in the repression of those whose lives compete with their own. For all that in the struggle of life are exposed to pain or fear, fill mankind with pity like his who came down from Heaven on account of the sorrows of the world. Jesus Christ our Lord." Major C W Hume

ALPHA AND OMEGA PRAYER

Christ, Jesus you are the beginning and the end. In You all things were created and in You all things are to be redeemed.

Christ Jesus, you are Lord of Creation. It was for all that You gave Your Life on the cross, a perfect sacrifice.

Take, now, to Your open arms our grief for your creation: for your wildlife, struggling against extinction; for the hunted and the trapped; for the abandoned and the homeless; for your food, animals unnaturally imprisoned, transported and slaughtered in terror; for your animals cruelly used as laboratory tools.

Christ Jesus, in us you live as Risen Lord and our hearts plead with You now to carry the pain of your suffering creatures, even to the last of these. The darkness of the world binds them as it bonds us. O Lord, and only your love can free us to live in Your light.

Christ Jesus, come. Redeem Your world. Amen.

May Tripp

SCRIPTURE READINGS

Suitable for Animal Welfare Services

or

Private Meditation

Genesis 1:20-31

Genesis 9:8-17

Numbers 22:20-35

Isaiah 11:1-9

Psalm 36:5-10

Psalm 104:1-30

Matthew 6:19-34

Mark 11:1-11

Luke 12:1-7

John 10:1-16

Romans 8:18-25

Revelation 4:2-11

Revelation 5:1-14

The following details of organisations listed by James are very likely to have changed

CARING GROUPS AND USEFUL ADDRESSES

(THOSE INVOLVED IN PRAYER, BIBLICAL MEDITATION AND ACTION)

INTERDENOMINATIONAL

(1) ANIMAL CHRISTIAN CONCERN
46 St. Margaret's Road,
Horsforth, Leeds.
LS18 5BG.

(2) FELLOWSHIP OF LIFE
Mrs. M. E. Lawson,
Nirvana, 12 Argyle Street,
Inverness. IV2 3BA.

(3) THE ORDER OF THE CROSS
10 De Vere Gardens,
Kensington,
London. W8 5AE.

DENOMINATIONAL

(4) ANGLICAN SOCIETY FOR THE WELFARE OF ANIMALS
10 Chester Avenue,
Hawkesbury, Tunbridge Wells,
Kent.

(5) CATHOLIC STUDY CIRCLE FOR ANIMAL WELFARE
39 Onslow Gardens,
London. E.18.

(6) QUAKER CONCERN FOR ANIMAL WELFARE
c/o Webbs Cottage,
Saling, Braintree,
Essex. CM7 5DZ.

Each of the numbered may be remembered in prayer, following a six day cycle; or, allowing for those that follow, a monthly rota could be adhered to.

CARING GROUPS OF ALL SHADES

(7) ANIMAL VIGILANTES, James Mason House, 24 Salisbury Street, Fordingbridge, Hants. SP6 1AF.

(8) ANIMAL AID, 7 Castle Street, Tonbridge, Kent. TN9 1BH.

(9) BLUE CROSS ANIMALS' HOSPITAL, Hugh Street, Victoria, London. SW1V 1QQ.

(10) B.U.A.V., 16a Crane Grove, Islington, London. N7 8LB.

(11) C.I.V.I.T.A.S., P.O. Box 338, London. E8 2AL.

(12) CHICKEN'S LIB., P.O. Box 2, Holmfirth, Huddersfield, HD7 1QT.

(13) C.I.W.F., 20 Lavant Street, Petersfield, Hampshire.

(14) C.A.A.C.A., Humane Education Centre, Avenue Lodge, Bounds Green Road, London. N22 4EN.

(15) C.P.C.A., P.O. Box 14, Romsey. SO5 9NN.

(16) GREENPEACE., Graham Street, London. N1.

(17) H.S.A., P.O. Box 19, London. S.E.22.

(18) I.C.A.B., 13 Greystone Road, Tankerton, Nr. Whitstable, Kent. CT5 2J4.

(19) I.F.A.W., Tubwell House, New Road, Crowborough, East Sussex. TN6 2HQ.

(20) N.A.V.S. & LORD DOWDING FUND, 51 Harley Street, London. W1N 1DD.

(21) N.E.S.A.D.L., Oak Tree Farm, Wetheral Shields, Carlisle. CA4 8JA.

(22) N.S.A.C.S., 33 Forest Rise, Jarvis Brook, Crowborough, East Sussex. TN6 2EP.

(23) P.D.S.A., P.D.S.A. House, South Street, Dorking, Surrey. RH4 2LB.

(24) PETWATCH, P.O. Box 16, Brighouse, West Yorkshire.

(25) R.S.P.B., The Lodge, Sandy, Bedfordshire. SG19 2DL.

(26) S.S.P.C.A., 19 Melville Street, Edinburgh. EH3 7PL.

(27) S.A.V.S., 121 West Regent Street, Glasgow. G2 2SD.

(28) S.S.P.V. & ST. ANDREW ANIMAL FUND, 10 Queensferry Street, Edinburgh. EH12 4PG.

(29) ZOO CHECK, Cherry Tree Cottage, Coldharbour, Nr. Dorking. RH5 6HA.

POLITICAL GROUPS

(30) CONSERVATIVE ANTI-HUNT COUNCIL, 3 London Rd., Luton. LU1 3UE.

LIBERAL ANIMAL WELFARE GROUP, 16 Valingers Rd., King's Lynn.

A POEM AND A PRAYER

"I know that every living thing
is here in its own right
That He who made an insect's wings
delights to see it's flight
Who treats a fly with cruelty
God's purposes denies
Lord may I always gentle be
to everything that flies
I know that all that breathes and moves
is precious in Your sight
The creatures that the sunshine loves,
the beasts that prowl at night
Lord may I show true courtesy
 to all whose ways are mild
And always show true chivalry
to creatures of the wild"

With acknowledgements to an unknown author.
submitted by Ruby Haley who, both deaf and blind,
sings it to 'Crimond'!

THE COMPILER

James Thompson is a militant advocate of animal welfare in and out of the church. In the past he has represented the Dean of Westminster in handing relevant petitions to 10 Downing Street; while animal activists have asked him to address a gathering of no less than eleven thousand.

James's compassion for the animals has never been at the expense of human need; his recent role has been that of a Senior Hospital Chaplain in Aberdeen. He is also Honorary Chaplain for Scotland of the leading Christian Singles Group which caters for the lonely, separated, divorced and bereft.

He is a strong supporter of alternative medicine whose ethical standards, as well as research for scientific accuracy, will not permit vivisection; and is a bona fide hypno analyst and psychotherapist.

A qualified lecturer as well as a recent member of Grampian Regional Education Committee James accepts, at mere nominal expense engagements from far and wide to further the animal cause, to awaken decent folk to the barbarities inflicted on animals under emotive terms such as "cancer research" and "research into Aids".

"No ultimate good will come out of an evil deed" were the words uttered to him by his mother when he was 17. Turning 58 he sees the truth of her philosophy clearer than ever.

****

James's heartfelt thanks are extended to his wife Doreen and his friends Jill Russell and David Bennett as well as each contributor without whom this publication would not have been possible.

£2.28

The Live Exports Prayer

by Pastor James

Gracious Father, we ask for your guidance and blessing over the farming communities of Wales. We realise that they have undergone much heartache and pain and so we ask for guidance concerning their future lives.
 The Holy Bible tells us that what we sow must eventually reap. So just as harvest time follows a time of sowing, so we pray, today, that your children will sow compassion and care to all forms of life committed to their care.
 We feel, Dear God, that husbandry over weaker forms of life has become far removed today from what it was when Jesus walked this earth; so we pray that the kindness and care shepherds once displayed towards their sheep might return to this lovely land of Wales.
 As Jesus told of how a good shepherd will lay down his own life to protect sheep committed to his charge, so today may the farmers of Wales show a similar deep concern and care for the lambs and calves committed to them.
 Teach us to realise that to subject these defenceless and gentle creatures, to any future stress and deprivation; the denial of their God given instincts – for no higher a reason or motive than to satisfy the acquired carnivorous palate of a distant gourmet – is surely unforgivable and inexcusable.

 Help us to remember that we, ourselves, could have been born an animal; for there are far more of them than there are of us! Who knows? – for our just desserts our future existence: the hell our Saviour so solemnly warned us of, could be a future existence as one of these.
 Father, we do not claim to have the answers; we only know that to have been born as a human – shall we say; this time round? – is a most awesome responsibility indeed; for as humans we alone have the ability to bless or blight the creation which you made us guardians and stewards.
 Father, we pray for your blessing upon the sheep, and other creatures, you have entrusted to our protection. May we, like Jesus, lead the sheep by calm and still waters – especially the ewes who are with young; and may we take up the lambs, as He did, keeping them close to our breast. Indeed,

when they hear our voice may they come to us because they recognise our love for them; knowing that whatever we do it will be for their constant welfare and care.

May the people of Wales show their true mettle. May they rise up to put compassion and protection of weaker forms of life, before selfishness, greed and monetary gain, for – as the Good Shepherd Himself said: 'What will it profit a man if he gains the whole world yet, through it, lose his very soul?'.

This prayer we offer in the Name of the Good Shepherd, The Lamb of God, Jesus Christ Our Lord.

Amen

James and Doreen at 'Peacehaven' January 2008

Remembrance Day 2012 service at the
Animals At War Memorial, London

Lightning Source UK Ltd.
Milton Keynes UK
UKHW021008041122
411565UK00009B/93